a journal of vexillology

RUSSIAN REGIONAL FLAGS

*Flags of the Subjects
of the Russian Federation*

ANNE M. PLATOFF

Edward B. Kaye, Editor

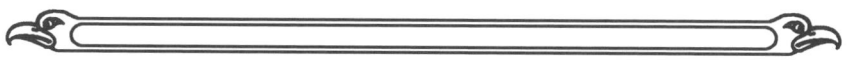

North American Vexillological Association
Volume 16 — 2009

Subscriptions & Submission of Articles

Raven: A Journal of Vexillology is published by the North American Vexillological Association (NAVA), PMB 225, 1977 North Olden Avenue Extension, Trenton, New Jersey 08618-2193, USA. Address manuscripts and correspondence concerning them to the attention of the *Raven* editor. Address subscription/membership questions to the attention of the Membership Committee.

Submission of Articles: For guidelines and schedule, contact the *Raven* editor, c/o NAVA. Send a paper copy of the article to the *Raven* editor, along with copies of any photographs or figures plus the text on computer disk in WordPerfect or MS Word with a minimum of formatting. (To have the material returned, include a self-addressed envelope with sufficient postage.) Articles are subject to an annual juried review and accepted based on criteria set by the Editorial Board. Authors of accepted articles must sign a publication agreement assigning copyright to NAVA and affirming that the material is original and not previously published elsewhere. Articles will be edited for style, consistency, and length.

Material appearing in *Raven* does not necessarily reflect the policy or opinion of NAVA, the NAVA executive board, or the *Raven* editor.

Information concerning permission to reprint articles is available from the *Raven* editor. Articles appearing in *Raven* are abstracted and indexed in *HISTORICAL ABSTRACTS* and *AMERICA: HISTORY AND LIFE.*

Raven: A Journal of Vexillology
© 2009 North American Vexillological Association. All rights reserved.
ISSN 1071-0043   ISBN: 978-0-9747728-2-0
Printed in USA

RAVEN

Volume 16 — 2009

CONTENTS

Russian Regional Flags

Introduction	1
Acknowledgments	4
The Russian Federation	5
Design Analysis	
Design Basics	10
Colors Used in the Flags	12
Symbols	18
Summary	31
Flag Descriptions	
Federal Subjects	33
Merged Federal Subjects	129
Conclusion	139
Contributors	141
Index	143

NAVA gratefully acknowledges the financial support for this volume provided by the University of California, Santa Barbara Library (where the author works), the Vexillological Association of the State of Texas (which organized the NAVA annual meeting where this book was first presented as a paper), and Peter Ansoff (past president of NAVA and frequent contributor to *Raven*).

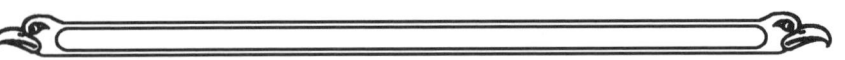

Illustration Credits

Images of the current flags and coats of arms were taken from the compact disk *Russian Regional Heraldry / Regional'naia simvolika Rossii*, purchased from Vector-Images.com. Images of most obsolete flags were purchased from the website http://www.vector-images.com. In some cases the colors vary from images on the websites of the federal subjects. This is most obvious in the various shades of blue used (see the discussion in the Color section). On three flags the stripes are described as "silver", but are shown as white or very light gray in the images—Ivanovo Oblast, Kaluga Oblast, and Kursk Oblast. It is also quite common for a color to be described as "gold", but represented on the flag in yellow. In addition, some flags are not depicted in their official proportions.

Territorial maps were obtained from Wikimedia Commons (http://commons.wikimedia.org) and were contributed to the commons by Marmelad.

*This book is dedicated to
Michael Platoff
for his love and support.*

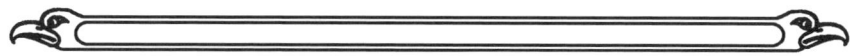

NAVA

The North American Vexillological Association (NAVA) is a nonprofit organization dedicated to the promotion of vexillology, the scientific and scholarly study of flag history and symbolism. Its members come from all fields of vexillology, including flag collectors and historians, government officials, museum directors, and flag manufacturers and retailers, as well as those interested in flags as a hobby. NAVA publishes *Raven: A Journal of Vexillology* and a newsletter, *NAVA News,* hosts the website www.nava.org, holds annual meetings, undertakes special projects, and participates in international vexillological events.

For membership information, contact the Membership Committee, North American Vexillological Association, PMB 225, 1977 North Olden Avenue Extension, Trenton, New Jersey 08618-2193, USA, or visit www.nava.org.

2008–2009 Executive Board

Hugh L. Brady, *President*	Austin, Texas
Gustavo Tracchia, *First Vice President*	Kew Gardens, New York
Anne M. Platoff, *Second Vice President*	Goleta, California
William J. Trinkle, *Secretary*	Sacramento, California
Edward B. Kaye, *Treasurer*	Portland, Oregon

Editorial Board

Scot M. Guenter, Ph.D.	San José State University
Anne M. Platoff, M.S., M.A.	University of California, Santa Barbara
John M. Purcell, Ph.D.	Cleveland State University, *Emeritus*

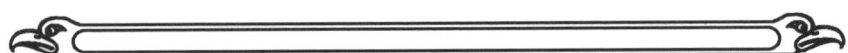

Introduction

For English-speaking vexillologists there are very few sources of information about the subnational flags of the Russian Federation. Probably the most thorough source is the website *FOTW: Flags of the World*. While an excellent site for flag information, the entries are not always current and it is sometimes difficult to trace information back to an original source. In addition, the level of detail for different flags varies widely. It is often difficult to tell if the information contained is a comprehensive treatment of all information available on a flag, or just what the contributor could find at the time.

F. I. Sharkov's bilingual book *Vetry peremen: flagi i gerby respublik Rossii / Winds of Change: Flags and Coats of Arms of the Russian Republics* provides some text in English about the flags of the Russian republics. However, it was published in 1992 and is out of date. In addition, it contains no information on the other federal subjects—the oblasts, krais, autonomous oblast, autonomous okrugs, and federal cities. Therefore it is far from a comprehensive treatment of the flags of all the federal subjects of Russia.

The purpose of this work is to present a discussion of all of the subnational flags of the Russian Federation, updated to 2009, in English. To do this, I have consulted a number of Russian-language sources to find explanations of symbolism, information about designs and history of the flags, and any other available information.

In the process of doing this, I realized just how little I (and, perhaps, most Westerners) really know about the territories of the modern Russian Federation. It was fascinating to discover just what could be learned about a place and its people from the flag they have chosen and the meaning that they have assigned to it. So, in addition to providing updated information about flags and symbolism, I have examined what this information can teach about the peoples and territories of Russia, and about the world's largest country—the Russian Federation.

Transliteration and Capitalization of Russian Words

Author-produced transliterations use the Library of Congress transliteration system for Russian. Citations to English-language sources using transliteration are cited according to the transliteration scheme used in the original. This accounts for variations in transliteration in the notes. According to the LC transliteration system, Russian letters (in alphabetical order) are represented as follows:

А,а: A,a	К,к: K,k	Х,х: Kh,kh
Б,б: B,b	Л,л: L,l	Ц,ц: Ts,ts
В,в: V,v	М,м: M,m	Ч,ч: Ch,ch
Г,г: G,g	Н,н: N,n	Ш,ш: Sh,sh
Д,д: D,d	О,о: O,o	Щ,щ: Shch,shch
Е,е: E,e	П,п: P,p	ъ: "
Ё,ё: Ë,ë	Р,р: R,r	ы: y
Ж,ж: Zh,zh	С,с: S,s	ь: '
З,з: Z,z	Т,т: T,t	Э,э: E,e
И,и: I,i	У,у: U,u	Ю,ю: Iu,iu
Й,й: I,i	Ф,ф: F,f	Я,я: Ia,ia

In other systems yo is used instead of ë, yu instead of iu, and ya instead of ia.

All transliterated names, phrases, and titles in the text and in the notes use the Russian rules of capitalization, which capitalize fewer words than would be standard in English. However, in the English text the standard English rules of capitalization are applied to Russian place names.

Geographic Names and Terms

To make the text more readable, the Russian geographical terms "oblast", "krai", and "okrug" have only been italicized on the first use where they are defined, but not for any following instances of use. Also, these terms are not translated in the text as they are commonly used in English-language texts about Russia. This practice will keep the geographic names closer to the original language. The majority of Russian place names throughout the text are stated using one of the conventional spellings from *Merriam-Webster's Geographical Dictionary* (2001), which uses the transliteration standard of the United States Board on Geographic Names. In a few cases, common usage has varied from the most current edition, so I have chosen to use the more common forms of the names. For example, the dictionary uses the spelling "kray" rather than "krai" for that type of federal subject. In this work, it made more sense to use "krai". Also, there is a lot of variation in the English forms of the names for the autonomous okrugs. In the flag description section, common names in English are followed by the official name in Russian, and then transliterated Russian using the LC transliteration scheme.

Republics are typically called just by their place names, but other federal subjects will be called by their full names to avoid confusion with cities of the same names.

Flag Descriptions

As much as possible, flag descriptions and symbolism have been drawn from the text on the official websites of the federal subjects. Where information was not available from the federal subjects, secondary sources (primarily in Russian) have been used.

The descriptions are not direct translations, but are instead English-language descriptions based upon a variety of Russian-language sources. In some cases translation has been challenging, as some Russian words can be translated using various terms in English. Wherever possible, I have attempted to use the term that I felt most appropriately described the flag and symbolism in English.

Acknowledgments

I wish to thank the following people for their invaluable assistance and advice in the completion of this project: Lydia Agadjanova, Sherri Barnes, Richard Caldwell, Mikhail Egorov, Jane Faulkner, Chuck Huber, Ted Kaye, Roman Klimeš, Mary Larsgaard, Victor Lomantsov, Janet Martorana, Katia McClain, Larry McLellan, John Purcell, Mikhail Revnivtsev, Charles Spain, and Yen Tran.

Thanks also go out to the employees of BIAR Natsional'naia Simvolika and their stores in Moscow (yl. Pervomaiskaia) and St. Petersburg. Their patience with a visiting vexillologist from America trying to buy a collection of flags was essential to the initiation of this project. And special thanks to BIAR employee Anton Kuprin for recommending a place to buy the flags during my visit to Russia, and for helping me to complete the set once I returned home.

Finally, this project would not have been possible without the love and support of my husband, Michael Platoff. He accompanied me on two major flag-shopping excursions in Russia, supported the purchase of many flag books and images from Russia, provided feedback throughout the process, and demonstrated an amazing amount of patience.

Additional thanks go to the UC Santa Barbara Library, the Vexillological Association of the State of Texas (VAST), and Peter Ansoff for generously providing funding for the addition of color plates to this volume of *Raven*.

Anne M. Platoff

The Russian Federation

The breakup of the Soviet Union was a pivotal event in modern vexillology. As each former Soviet republic asserted its own identity, old symbols were replaced and a number of new national flags were introduced. This was not the case for the Russian Federation, which reverted to traditional designs for its national symbols. The most dynamic aspect of modern Russian flags appears at the subnational level. This paper will examine the current flags of Russia's subdivisions, collectively known as "federal subjects", and will analyze design trends to draw conclusions about the new subnational flags of Russia.

Following the breakup of the Soviet Union in 1991, the 15 republics of the USSR each became independent states. By far the largest of those republics is the Russian Federation, the largest country in the world geographically with an area of 17 million square kilometers. It ranks ninth in the world in population, with 142 million people as of 1 January 2009. The Russian Federation is both a European and an Asian country—geographically, historically, and culturally. Its territory covers 40% of the European continent and spans all of northern Asia. The population of Russia is ethnically diverse—there are approximately 160 different ethnic groups in Russia, speaking over 100 languages. In fact, two words in the Russian language translate to "Russian" in English. The first, *russkii*, means ethnically Russian, while *rossiiskii* means someone who is a citizen of the Russian Federation. Thus, while all the citizens of Russia are *rossiiskii,* they are not all *russkii*. This diversity is reflected in the political subdivisions of Russia, as well as in their flags.[1]

---

1. "Russia", *Wikipedia*, http://en.wikipedia.org/wiki/Russian_federation, accessed 21 July 2008; *Merriam-Webster's Geographical Dictionary*, 3rd ed. (Springfield, Mass.: Merriam-Webster, 2001); "Geography", "Transliteration Systems" (Appendix 1), "Geographical Designations" (Appendix 2), in *The Russian Context: the Culture Behind the Language,* edited by Eloise M. Boyle and Genevra Gerhart (Bloomington, Ind.: Slavica, 2002), pp. 505-560; 633-640.

6 *Russian Regional Flags*

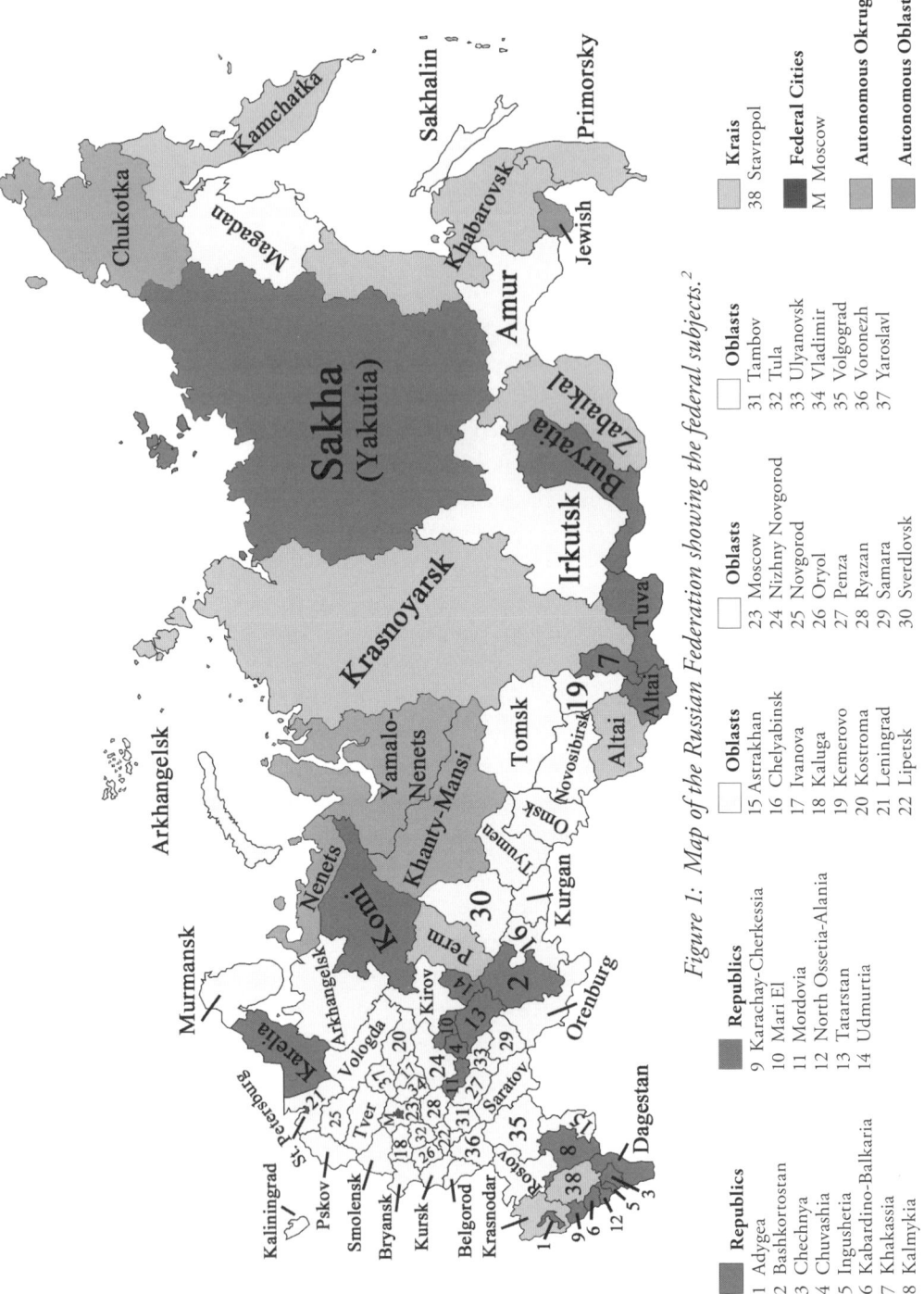

Figure 1: *Map of the Russian Federation showing the federal subjects.*[2]

2. Map of the federal subjects is based upon a map from the *Wikipedia Commons*, http://commons.wikimedia.org/wiki/Image:Russian-regions.png, accessed on 27 August 2008.

A short lesson in Russia's political geography is necessary for any study of its subnational flags. When the constitution of the Russian Federation was adopted in 1993, the country consisted of 89 subdivisions called "federal subjects". Since that time several of these geographic units have been consolidated so that, effective 1 March 2008 there are now 83 federal subjects in the Russian Federation. Each is represented by two deputies in the *Sovet Federatsii* (Federation Council), the upper house of Russia's parliament—the *Federal'noe Sobranie* (Federal Assembly), so in terms of representation at the federal level, they are equal. However, different types of federal subjects enjoy different levels of autonomy.

The federal subjects with the highest level of autonomy are the republics. According to the Russian constitution, each of the 21 republics can adopt its own constitution and establish a national language (to be used in addition to the Russian language). Each republic also has an elected president and parliament. While republics are meant to be a home to a specific ethnic group (called the titular nationality), that group does not always constitute a majority of the population in that region. During the Soviet period most of the current republics were Autonomous Soviet Socialist Republics (ASSRs) within the Russian Soviet Federative Socialist Republic (Russian SFSR). There are also several regions that were classified as autonomous oblasts in the Russian SFSR, but are now republics of the Russian Federation. While the formal names of these federal subjects include the word "republic", in everyday usage they are usually called by their common names.[3]

There are currently 9 *krais* (usually translated as "territories" and often spelled "kray" in English) and 46 *oblasts* (usually translated as "provinces") in the Russian Federation. These subdivisions are basically the same in terms of autonomy. Each has a federally-appointed governor and a locally-elected parliament. Most oblasts and krais are named after the largest city in the region. For this reason, it becomes important to differentiate between the federal subjects and their namesake cities by using the word "oblast" or "krai". The krais were historically considered frontier regions and have retained the designation of "territory" in recognition of this status.[4]

---

3. "Federal Subjects of Russia", *Wikipedia*, http://en.wikipedia.org/wiki/Federal_subjects_of_russia, accessed 1 May 2008; "Federativnoe ustroistvo Rossii", *Vikipediia*, no direct URL available, accessed 1 May 2008; "Republics of Russia", *Wikipedia*, http://en.wikipedia.org/wiki/Republics_of_Russia, accessed 1 May 2008.

4. "Federal Subjects of Russia", *Wikipedia*, http://en.wikipedia.org/wiki/Federal_subjects_of_russia, accessed 1 May 2008; "Federativnoe ustroistvo Rossii", *Vikipediia*, no direct URL available, accessed 1 May 2008.

The Russian Federation currently includes one autonomous oblast and four autonomous *okrugs* (usually translated as "districts"). The lone autonomous oblast is the Jewish Autonomous Oblast. This region was established in 1934 as a secular home for the Jews of the Soviet Union and was intended as a center of Yiddish culture. Ironically, today the Jewish residents of this region constitute only about 1.2% of the population. The autonomous okrugs are ethnic homelands which are usually encircled by an oblast or krai, although one is not within another federal subject. When the 1993 constitution was adopted, there were 10 autonomous okrugs, but six of them have since been consolidated into their oblasts/krais and only four retain their status as federal subjects.[5]

Finally, there are two metropolitan areas designated as "cities of federal importance", or federal cities. They are the largest cities in Russia—Moscow and St. Petersburg. These cities enjoy the status of "federal subjects", but they do not have the same level of autonomy as most of the other federal subjects. While they are surrounded by oblasts, they are not technically part of those oblasts.[6]

It is also important to note that all federal subjects, regardless of their level of autonomy, are considered an inherent part of the Russian Federation and according to the constitution their status cannot change without the consent of the Russian government. While some regions might desire more than their current level of autonomy, it is unlikely that any of the federal subjects will be allowed to seek independence in the near future.[7]

The majority of federal subjects had no historical flags when the Russian Federation became an independent country, although in many cases historical arms could be used as a basis for their new symbols. During the period of the Russian Empire and the chaos following the revolution, several of the current Russian republics briefly enjoyed status as independent countries and had their own flags, but few of those designs have gained status as federal subject flags. In fact, most of the subdivisions of the Russian Federation have long histories as territories of

---

5. *Ibid.*; "Autonomous Okrugs of Russia", *Wikipedia*, http://en.wikipedia.org/wiki/Autonomous_okrugs_of_Russia, accessed 1 May 2008.

6. "Federal Subjects of Russia", *Wikipedia*, http://en.wikipedia.org/wiki/Federal_subjects_of_russia, accessed 1 May 2008; "Federativnoe ustroistvo Rossii", *Vikipediia*, no direct URL available, accessed 1 May 2008.

7. *The Territories of the Russian Federation 2007* (London: Routledge, 2007); Boyle and Gerhart, pp. 505-560; 633-640; "Federal Subjects of Russia," *Wikipedia*, http://en.wikipedia.org/wiki/Federal_subjects_of_russia, accessed 1 May 2008; "Federativnoe ustroistvo Rossii", *Vikipediia*, no direct URL available, accessed 1 May 2008.

Russia. The old imperial subdivisions, known as *guberniyas* and *oblasts*, typically had arms but not flags. In the Soviet period, while each or the 15 Soviet Republics had its own flag, the only subdivisions of the Russian SFSR with flags were the Autonomous Soviet Socialist Republics. Their flags consisted of the Russian SFSR flag with the initials of the autonomous republic underneath the hammer and sickle.

Only after the creation of the Russian Federation did most federal subjects have the opportunity to create and adopt their own flags. The new flag designs that have emerged are as diverse as the federal subjects themselves. Some are completely new, but the majority of the designs are drawn from the historical symbols of the regions. In fact, many of the oblast coats of arms are directly related to the historical arms of their namesake cities, and this has in turn influenced the flag designs. In summary, the modern flags of the federal subjects are for the most part completely new since 1991, while still heavily influenced by the heraldry and some flag designs of the past.

Design Analysis

The flags of Russia's federal subjects reveal trends in flag design when studied and analyzed. Each flag was investigated to confirm that it was, indeed, an official flag of the region. In several cases a flag shown on a website or in a flag catalog was not an official symbol and the federal subject had not yet adopted a flag. In addition, with the consolidations that have occurred since 2005 the status of some flags has become unclear. Several consolidated territories have continued to use the flag of the main territory or district, while others have formed commissions to work on new symbols. As of 23 September 2009, 81 of the 83 federal subjects had officially adopted flags. These 81 were considered in this design analysis.

Design Basics

Examination of the flags and coats of arms of the federal subjects reveal an interesting trend in subnational flag designs of the modern Russian Federation. While the vast majority of the flag designs were created since 1991, the legacy of traditional Russian heraldry is quite evident. Of the 81 federal subjects with flags, 66 (81%) of them have flags based at least in part upon their coats of arms. Seven flags (9%) are armorial banners which replicate the shields of the arms. Another 24 (30%) incorporate the full coat of arms into the designs. Most numerous are the flags that include at least one element from the arms—35 flags or 43% of all flags.

To identify other trends in flag design, the 81 flags initially were divided into four basic categories: solid fields, striped fields, quartered/crossed flags, and diagonally-divided fields. The majority of the flags (72%) have striped designs. There are also a significant number with solid fields (22%). Four flags are quartered or crossed, and one flag is divided into diagonal stripes. In addition, five flags have triangles at the hoist, one of these has a solid field and four are striped.

Basic Designs	Flags	Percentage
Solid fields	18	22%
Striped fields	58	72%
Quartered/crossed	4	5%
Diagonally-divided	1	1%
[Triangle at hoist also]	[5]	[6%]

Figure 2. Basic designs of the flags of the Federal Subjects.

Of the striped flags, 46 include charges and 12 have no additional symbols other than the stripes. There are many more horizontal than vertical stripes. On 14% of the striped flags a single vertical stripe is at either the hoist or fly. Four of the striped flags also have triangles at the hoist.

Striped Flag Designs	Flags	Percentage of Striped Flags
With symbols	46	79%
Without symbols	12	21%
Horizontal	44	76%
Vertical	15	26%
Single stripe at hoist/fly	8	14%
Triangle at hoist	4	7%

Figure 3. Striped flags by category.

The national flag of Russia is both a tribar flag and a tricolor flag. Tribars are divided into three stripes—horizontally, vertically, or diagonally. On the Russian flag the stripes are horizontal. Tricolor refers to the fact that the flag has a field of three colors. Both tribar and tricolor designs are popular worldwide, and the same is true of the federal subjects. Among the flags of the federal subjects, 20 are horizontal tribars and 17 are tricolors. In addition, three flags give the impression of horizontal tricolored tribar flags, except that some of their stripes are scalloped on the top edge.[8]

One final aspect of basic flag design that should be discussed is the proportions. Flag proportions are usually described as the ratio of the width of the flag

---

8. For more information on tribar flags, see "Triband (flag)", *Wikipedia*, http://en.wikipedia.org/wiki/Triband_(flag), accessed 27 August 2008; for more information on tricolors, see "Tricolour", *Wikipedia*, http://en.wikipedia.org/wiki/Tricolour, accessed 27 August 2008.

(measured top to bottom at the hoist) to the length of the flag (the distance from the hoist to the fly). Most of the flags of Russia's federal subjects use one of two proportions—1:2 or 2:3. Nearly a quarter use the ratio of 1:2, the proportions of the old Soviet flag. However, over the years a number of federal subjects have changed their flags to 2:3, the proportions of the current Russian tricolor, so that today the majority of Russia's subnational flags match the proportions of the national flag. Two of the federal subjects use unique proportions: the Republic of Chuvashia (5:8) and Penza Oblast (1:1.6).

Colors Used in the Flags

No study of flags would be complete without a discussion of the colors used. Color is so significant that many flags use color alone for their symbolism. Determining which colors to count was not as easy as it might sound. One possible technique would have been to count only "field" colors, but this presented some issues. For example, consider a flag with a triangle at the hoist and two stripes at the fly—is the triangle a symbol or would that color count? What about the color of a large cross that extends to all four sides of the flag? A number of the flags include scalloped or wavy stripes representing water. Are these stripes symbols or are they part of the field? In some cases (such as that of Leningrad Oblast) it is clear that the wavy stripes are more than symbols; they are intended to present the image of a striped field. And what about fimbriation colors—should they be counted? The federal subjects tend to assign meaning to all the colors used, demonstrating that they are considered important to the design. So, rather than approaching the question strictly as a vexillologist, it was posed from the perspective of residents of the federal subject—if asked about the colors of their flag, what would they say? Using this point of view, all of the principal colors used in the fields of the flags were counted—those used in solid backgrounds, all stripes in the field, hoist triangles, crosses, and scalloped/wavy lines. Colors used in arms, symbols, and disks (since they are part of the symbols) were not counted. For example, the rainbow on the flag of the Jewish Autonomous Oblast was considered to be a symbol, rather than seven stripes, based on the consistency across various descriptions where the flag was described as white with a rainbow and color meanings were not assigned to the individual rainbow colors.

The flags of the federal subjects demonstrate variety in the number of colors used. 17 flags (21%) have only one color in their fields. Bicolored flags total 22, or 27% of all the flags. The influence of the national flag might well explain the number of flags which use three colors—35, or 43%. Finally, 7 flags (9%) use four or more colors.

Colors Used	Flags	Percentage
One	17	21%
Two	22	27%
Three	35	43%
Four or more	7	9%

Figure 4. Number of colors used.

Color choice in flags is influenced by a variety of factors. In every culture certain colors have specific significance and symbolism. This is true in ethnic Russian culture as well as in the cultures of Russia's many minority groups. Historical influences can also affect the color choice. The colors used in many flags of the federal subjects have been influenced by past flags of the Russian Empire and the Soviet Union, and by the current national flag of the Russian Federation. Each region of Russia has chosen its own flag colors, and each has assigned specific meanings or significance to those colors. While there is a great variety of meaning assigned to each color, and some meanings are assigned to more than one color, a number of trends emerged when the color symbolism was examined.

Color	Flags	Percentage
Red	55	69%
Blue	48	59%
White	45	56%
Green	25	31%
Yellow	16	20%
Black	3	4%
Silver	3	4%

Figure 5. Color usage in flags of the Federal Subjects.

Not surprisingly, red is used in the most flags—55 flags, or 69% of flag designs. For centuries, red has been an important color in ethnic Russian culture and has become the color most frequently used to represent the Russian people. In the Russian language the word for red is *krasnyi*, which originally meant "fair" or "beautiful". In modern Russian it now shares a root with the words *krasota* and *krasivyi* which mean "beauty" and "beautiful". For this reason, red has long been associated with beauty. Some flags also use red to represent love, feelings, mercy, and magnanimity. In some cases, red symbolizes labor, industry, economic development, and progress. For other flags it might stand for democracy and authority, or even antiquity and continuity. Red can also be used to symbolize creation, the sun, fire, warmth, energy, life, health, maturity, and vitality. Probably the most significant meaning of red in the flags is its association with defense of the homeland. On many flags red represents the blood spilled in specific battles fought on the territory, heroism of the veterans, and defense preparedness. Red is historically tied to traits such as strength, masculinity, courage, bravery, fearlessness, boldness, selflessness, steadfastness, loyalty, and military valor. The importance of red has been a consistent force in Russian symbolism throughout history. It was an important color in the symbols of Muscovy, it was used during the height of Russian Empire, it was the dominant color in the symbolism of the Soviet Union, and it is still used heavily today.[9]

Blue is also popular in Russian subnational flags, used in 48 flags (59%). Like red, blue has long-standing status in the national symbolism of Russia. It was used in flags of Russia during the imperial period and in the flag of the Russian SFSR during the Soviet period. Unlike most languages, Russian has two distinctive words for "blue"—*sinii*, meaning dark blue; and *goluboi,* meaning light blue. In the flag descriptions, most federal subjects distinguish between the two blues, using either one or the other. Of the 48 flags that use blue, 30 use *sinii*, 14 use *goluboi*, and 4 designate their shade of blue as *lazurnyi* (meaning "azure"). Some, however, list multiple blues in their descriptions indicating that the exact shade can vary. To complicate matters, one flag's *sinii* can resemble another flag's *goluboi*, resulting in a wide variety of blues.[10] There are a number of meanings assigned to the color blue in the flag symbolism of the federal subjects. One of the most common is to use blue to represent parts of the natural environment such as the sky or bodies of water—rivers, lakes, seas, and oceans. Blue is also used to represent concepts such as beauty, love, happiness, well-being, peace, harmony, calmness, gentleness, hope, and freedom. In addition, blue is used to symbolize purity,

---

9. Alexander and Barbara Pronin, *Russian Folk Arts* (South Brunswick, N.J.: A. S. Barnes and Co., 1975) p. 153; N. M. Shanskii, *Russian Word Formation* (Oxford: Pergamon Press, 1968), p. 39; Catherine A. Wolkonsky and Marianna A. Poltoratzky, *Handbook of Russian Roots* (New York: Columbia University Press, 1961), p. 161-163; Virve Sarapik, "Red: the Colour and the Word", *Folklore* v. 3 (1997), http://www.folklore.ee/folklore/vol3/red.htm, p. [13], accessed 17 July 2008; Olga Dmitrieva, "Color Associations", *Color Matters*, http://www.colormatters.com/research/ColorAssociations.pdf, accessed 17 July 2008.

10. Another complication is the usage of *goluboi* in post-Soviet Russian slang to mean "homosexual". Perhaps the official descriptions have avoided this connotation by stating the color is *sinii*, while still using a light-blue color in their flags.

cleanliness, chastity, lofty aspirations, honor, virtue, honesty, sincerity, fairness, faithfulness, loyalty, and respect.[11]

White (*belyi*) is the third most popular color used in the flags of the federal subjects. It often represents cleanliness or purity, either of the natural environment or of the thoughts and intentions of the people. Other concepts symbolized by white are peace, love, happiness, tranquility, modesty, morality, innocence, truth, frankness, perfection, wisdom, nobility, honor, honesty, or well-being. In the Buddhist regions, it is often used to represent the milk or dairy products central to cultural practices and purification ceremonies. Concepts such as heaven, spirituality, and good are also associated with white. In many flags across the Russian Federation white is used to represent aspects of the natural environment such as light, the fragility of the land, snowy open spaces, the long, harsh Russian winters, and the northern regions in general.

Red, blue, and white are the national colors of Russia. The three colors are said to come from the arms of Moscow—red is the field color of the shield in the arms, St. George's horse is white, and his cape is blue. Using these established colors, Peter I (the Great) designed the first Russian white/blue/red tricolors as naval flags in the late 1690s. The Russian tricolor gained official status as the national flag in 1705. In Russian, this flag is sometimes referred to as *BESIK*, an acronym for the order of the colors in Russian (*belyi, sinii,* and *krasnyi*). Following the breakup of the Soviet Union in 1991, the tricolor was officially adopted as the flag of the Russian Federation. In vexillology white, blue, and red have become known as the "Pan-Slavic colors" because the Russian tricolor influenced the flags of many other Slavic countries. Just as Peter's tricolored flag influenced other Slavic flags, its influence can also be seen on a number of the federal subjects' flags. Most notable are those of Leningrad Oblast and Ulyanovsk Oblast which both use modified Russian tricolors as the fields of their flags, with the lower stripes scalloped to rep-

---

11. Jonathan Winawer, Nathan Witthoft, Michael C. Frank, Lisa Wu, Alex R. Wade, and Lera Boroditsky, "Russian Blues Reveal Effects of Language on Color Discrimination", *PNAS: Proceedings of the National Academy of Sciences*, v. 104 #19 (May 8, 2007), p. 7780-7785, http://www.pnas.org/cgi/doi/10.1073/pnas.0701644104, accessed 17 July 2008; Greville Corbett and Gerry Morgan, "Colour Terms in Russian: Reflections of Typological Constraints in a Single Language", *Journal of Linguistics*, v. 24 (1988), p. 31-64; Galina V. Paramei, "Singing the Russian Blues: An Argument for Culturally Basic Color Terms", *Cross-Cultural Research*, v. 39 (2005), p. 10-38, http://ccr.sagepub.com/cgi/content/abstracts/39/1/10, accessed 17 July 2008; Brian James Baer, "Engendering Suspicion: Homosexual Panic in the Post-Soviet Detektiv", *Slavic Review*, v. 64 #1 (Spring 2005), p. 24-42.

resent waves. In all, the three national colors are the basis for 11 flags (14%), and have been combined with at least one additional color in 6 flags (7%).[12]

In addition, some federal subjects have shown their unity with Russia by using the color combinations of two other historic Russian flags which use just two of the three colors. The first of these is the flag of the Russian Soviet Federative Socialist Republic, which was red with a blue stripe at the hoist. Three current flags—those of Altai Krai, Kemerovo Oblast, and Vladimir Oblast—use the Russian SFSR flag as the basis of their designs. Two federal subjects (Kostroma Oblast and Voronezh Oblast) originally had flags of this type, but have since redesigned their flags. In all, the red/blue color combination is used in 15 flags (19%), often in combination with other colors. The second historical influence is the *Andreevskii* flag (white with a blue St. Andrew's cross)—the historic and current naval flag. Blue and white are combined (often with other colors) in 13 flags or 16% of the federal subjects. Many of these regions specifically cite this combination as representating their unity with the Russian Federation. The most notable examples of blue/white flags are those of the Altai Republic (which consists simply of blue and white stripes), and Arkhangelsk Oblast (which is based on the *Andreevskii* flag). In all, 45 of the 81 flags (56%) appear to have derived colors from the current and historic flags of Russia.[13]

After the national colors, the next most popular color is green *(zelënyi)*. A number of flags use green almost certainly because of its status as the traditional color of Islam. While it is difficult to get an exact count of practicing Muslims in Russia, in eight republics Islam is either the religion of the majority or there is a significant Muslim population—Bashkortostan and Tatarstan in the Volga-Urals region and Adygea, Chechnya, Dagestan, Ingushetia, Kabardino-Balkaria, and Karachay-Cherkessia in the Northern Caucasus region. The flags of all these republics include green. In other parts of Russia, green is used to represent the natural world—life, flora, the steppe, the taiga, meadows, fields, and forests. It is the color of spring and summer, so important after the long Russian winter.

---

12. Evgennii Vladimirovich Pchelov, "Gosudarstvennyi flag", in *Gosudarstvennye simvoly Rossii: gerb, flag, gimn* (Moskva: Russkoe slovo, 2004) p. 81-102; "Flag Rossiiskoi iperii", *Vexillographia: Flagi Rossii,* http://www.vexillographia.ru/russia/index.htm, accessed 16 July 2008; Viktor Nikolaevich Saprykov, *Gosudarstvennaia simvolika regionov Rossii* (Moskva: Parad, 2006) p. 4-7; "Russia", *FOTW Flags of the World,* http://www.crwflags.com/FOTW/flags/ru.htm, accessed 16 July 2008.

13. *Ibid.*

Green also represents concepts such as life, hope, plenty, freedom, peace, revival, renewal, friendship, brotherhood, joy, health, fertility, prosperity, stability, youth, vitality, wisdom, and eternal life.[14]

Another color with some religious significance is yellow *(zhëltyi)*. Like Islam in the Muslim republics, Buddhism has also played a role in color choices for the republics where that religion is practiced by the majority of the population. Most Buddhists in Russia practice Tibetan Buddhism, in which yellow has great religious significance. All three of the Buddhist republics—Buryatia, Kalmykia, and Tuva—have yellow in their flags. In other parts of the Russian Federation, yellow and gold are often considered synonymous in the descriptions of the flags. A number of meanings have been assigned to yellow/gold—peace, prosperity, spirituality, faith, happiness, health, well-being, wisdom, and knowledge. Because of its association with the color of ripe grain and the precious metal gold, yellow is frequently used to represent a rich harvest, abundance, prosperity, fertility, wealth, mineral resources, and good fortune. It is also used to symbolize greatness, power, durability, and constancy.[15]

Two other colors have been used in the flags of the federal subjects—black *(chërnyi)* and silver *(serebrianyi)*. Black represents stability, the land, and underground mineral wealth. It also symbolizes *chernozëm*—the rich black topsoil of central European Russia. In the portrayal of the flags, silver is often considered synonymous with white. It represents the concepts of light and purity of thoughts.

The colors used in the flags of the federal subjects reflect the diversity of the many regions of Russia, but they also link many of the regional flags to the country's history. In all, the array of subnational flags is both colorful and distinctive. The meanings assigned to these colors are equally diverse.

---

14. Galina M. Yemelianova, "Russia", in *Muslim Cultures Today* (Westport, Conn.: Greenwood Press, 2006) pp. 147-148; U.S. Department of State, "International Religious Freedom Report 2007", http://www.state.gov/g/drl/rls/irf/2007/90196.htm (14 September 2007), accessed 21 July 2008.

15. "Republic of Bashkortostan", p. 175-179; "Republic of Kalykiya", p. 148-150; "Republic of Tyva", p. 244-246. in *The Territories of the Russian Federation 2007*.

18 *Russian Regional Flags*

Symbols

A wide variety of symbols are used on the different flags of the federal subjects. In order to learn more about the types of symbols used, they were sorted into different categories. As some flags fit into multiple categories, they might be listed more than once.

Symbols of Russia, the Tsars, and Nobility

Figure 6. Symbols of the tsars and the Russian Empire on the flags of (from top to bottom) Kaluga Oblast, Tver Oblast, Kostroma Oblast, and Krasnodar Krai.

In 1991 the Russian Federation readopted the flag and coat of arms of imperial Russia. The major element of the arms is the double-headed eagle whose heads symbolize both the European and Asian nature of Russia. Each head of the eagle wears a crown and a third crown tops the arms. In its right talon, the eagle holds a scepter topped with a Russian eagle; in his left talon he holds an orb, another traditional symbol of royal authority. In the center of the eagle are the arms of Moscow, which portray St. George the Victorious slaying a dragon.

Six federal subjects place the eagle from the Russian arms on their flags. In other cases, the federal subjects use symbols representing the tsars to show their unity with Russia. There are 19 flags with crowns in their arms. In addition, four flags have crowns as their principal symbols—those of Astrakhan Oblast, Kaluga Oblast, Tver Oblast, and Tyumen Oblast. The crowns on Tyumen Oblast's flag are stylized.

Orbs and scepters, traditional symbols of royal authority, are used on four flags (Vologda Oblast, Vladimir Oblast, Novgorod Oblast, and St. Petersburg). Thrones appear on the flags of Novgorod Oblast and Tver Oblast. The flag of Ryazan Oblast includes a prince as the central charge.

Imperial standards appear on three Russian subnational flags. An old imperial flag (gold with the Russian eagle) flies from the galleon on the flag of Kostroma Oblast and also appears on the arms of Orenburg Oblast. The flag of Krasnodar Krai has monogrammed banners of five rulers of the Russian Empire—Alexander I, Catherine II, Alexander II, Paul I, and Nicholas I. An imperial monogram—that of Empress Elizabeth Petrovna—appears on the flag of Kaliningrad Oblast.

Religious Symbols

Since the breakup of the Soviet Union and the discontinuance of the "official atheism" of that era, there has been a resurgence of religion in the Russian Federation. This not only includes Russian Orthodoxy, the traditional religion of pre-Soviet Russia, but other religions which have been practiced in various regions for centuries. As a result, a number of flags of the federal subjects include religious symbols.

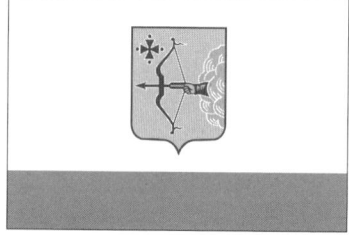

Christian symbols are the most common religious elements on the flags, especially crosses. They frequently appear on crowns or orbs, as a separate element in the arms, or as tall crosses borne by animals on the shields. Stavropol Krai's flag has a map of the region with a white cross marking the city of Stavropol as the religious center of the region. It also reflects the city's name—a Russified version of the Greek phrase meaning "The City of the Cross". A cross also tops the book of the Gospels which Perm Krai's bear carries upon its back, and is on the cover of the book as well. In addition, crosses divide the fields of Perm Krai, Stavropol Krai, Arkhangelsk Oblast, and Belgorod Oblast.

Figure 7. Christian symbolism on the flags of (from top to bottom) Kirov Oblast, Perm Krai, and Penza Oblast.

Religious figures also appear on several flags. The flags of Kirov Oblast and Volgograd Oblast show arms and hands extending from the clouds of heaven to bestow symbols of power and authority. Two flags (Moscow Oblast and the city of Moscow) feature St. George the Victorious, the patron saint of the region. Also, the flag of Arkhangelsk Oblast includes the Archangel Michael in the arms.

20 *Russian Regional Flags*

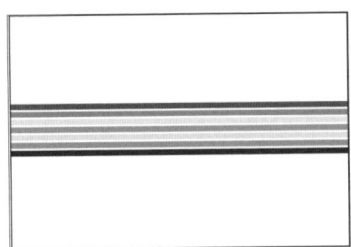

Figure 8: The rainbow, a biblical symbol, on the flag of (top) the Jewish Autonomous Oblast. The lotus, a traditional Buddhist symbol, on the flag of (center) Kalmykia. A cross symbolizing Russian Orthodoxy and the crescent moon representing Islam combined on the flag of Orenburg Oblast.

Perhaps the most striking depiction of Christian symbols, however, appears on the flag of Penza Oblast. This flag includes the face of Jesus from an icon called *"Spas Nerukotvornyi"* ("Our Savior Not Made by Hands"). The icon is based upon an orthodox tradition revolving around the Image of Edessa—a miraculous likeness of the face of Jesus which appeared on a rectangle of cloth, and is considered the first icon. It is also important to remember that icons are believed to take on the qualities of the saint portrayed. Therefore, the religious significance of this image of Christ transforms the flag itself into a type of icon. The flag also continues an old Russian tradition of using images of icons on flags. During the imperial period such flags were carried into battle by the troops of the Russian Empire.[16]

In addition to Christian symbols, symbols from other religions appear. For example, the Jewish Autonomous Oblast includes a rainbow on its flag—an Old Testament symbol of peace, happiness, and good. The seven stripes in the rainbow also represent the seven candles of a menorah, an important religious and cultural symbol of the Jewish people.

Buddhist symbolism appears on the flag of Kalmykia, which includes a white lotus flower—an important religious symbol for the people of the region because of its association with the life and teachings of the Buddha. The flower is one of the eight auspicious symbols and represents enlightenment. For this reason, the Buddha is often pictured sitting on a giant lotus flower.

The arms of Orenburg Oblast, which also appear on its flag, include both an Orthodox cross and a crescent moon. While most residents are Christian, approximately 20% of the population is Muslim. The other crescent moon appearing

---

16. *Simvoly i regalia Rossii* (Moskva: AST, 2006), p. 128-137; Alfredo Tradigo, *Icons and Saints of the Eastern Orthodox Church* (Los Angeles: The J. Paul Getty Museum, 2004), p. 6-7, 234-239.

on one of the flags is part of the *soyombo* symbol on Buryatia's flag. This region is predominantly Buddhist, and the *soyombo* is considered a cultural symbol rather than a religious one.

Plants and Animals

A number of Russian subnational flags include plants and animals among their symbols. Many of the plants are in the form of wreaths which surround the shields in coats of arms. Wreath materials used include laurel, oak, and cedar branches as well as cereal grains—a popular theme in Soviet arms symbolizing agricultural productivity. Several flags of the federal subjects have retained this symbol, most notably Altai Krai, which has a large stalk of grain in a stripe at the hoist. Oryol Oblast and Kemerovo Oblast include stalks of grain as elements on the shields of their arms. One of the most prominent plants on the flags is the linden tree on the flag of Lipetsk Oblast. A spruce tree is the primary symbol on the arms on the flag of Bryansk Oblast. In addition, the Republic of Chuvashia also has a tree, but it is in the form of a highly-stylized Tree of Life. Several flags use flowers as their primary symbols—the Republic of Kalmykia has a large lotus flower and the Republic of Bashkortostan uses a stylized *kurai* flower.

Animals appear on 28 of Russia's subnational flags. All of these are drawn from the arms of the regions, with the majority being animals which appear on the shields of the arms. A number of the flags have wild animals—five have lions, three have bears, one has a tiger, and another has a deer. There are also flags with domesticated animals—one with a camel, three with horses, and one with a goat. Two flags include fur-bearing animals important to the culture of Russia—sables and martens. Eagles appear on eight flags (including

Figure 9. Animals from the flags of (from top to bottom) Yaroslavl Oblast (bear), Primorsky Krai (tiger), Chelyabinsk Oblast (camel), and Novosibirsk Oblast (sables).

six with double-headed eagles). In addition, one flag has partridges, three have fish, and another includes bees. Three of the flags show mythical animals—two have dragons (being killed by St. George) and one has a bird from Slavic mythology called a *gamayun*.

Perhaps the most unique animal on any of the flags, however, is the *babr* on the flag of Irkutsk Oblast. On first glance the animal looks as if it might be a large member of the *mustelidae* (or weasel) family. It is obviously carnivorous since it has a dead sable in its mouth. However, it looks quite different from a wolverine or badger. The *babr* is black with a head and body that look almost feline; its feet appear to be webbed, and it has a broad flattened tail. A little linguistic research reveals this animal's unique history. Apparently the word *babr* is an obsolete Russian word for tiger. In fact, an examination of the arms of the city of Irkutsk from 1790 clearly shows a tiger with a sable in its mouth. So, how did the *babr* become transformed to its current appearance? As the story goes, when the arms of various territories were being revised in Moscow in 1857 the unfamiliar word *babr* was replaced by the more familiar word *bobr*, which means beaver. The result was a strange black animal, part feline and part beaver. It is interesting that, despite the obvious error, this form of the *babr* is still being used. Perhaps it has been retained because of its distinctiveness.

Figure 10. The babrs *from the city arms (left) of Irkutsk (1790) and the arms of Irkutsk Oblast (today).*

People, Body Parts, and Human Images

Eight flags include people, body parts, or human images among their symbols. Ryazan Oblast's flag shows a prince from the arms of the territory. The flag of Volgograd Oblast includes a statue of Mother Russia called *Rodina-mat' zovet* (which generally translates as "The Motherland Calls"). All of the other flags include images of religious significance. Two of the flags (Moscow Oblast and that of the city of Moscow) include the patron saint of Moscow, St. George the Victorious, on his horse slaying a dragon. The Archangel Michael is shown vanquish-

Figure 11. Figures on the flags of Ryazan Oblast (left) and Volgograd Oblast.

ing a demon in the arms on Arkhangelsk Oblast's flag. Penza Oblast's flag has an image of the face of Jesus from an icon called *"Spas Nerukotvornyi"*. According to Orthodox tradition, a miraculous image of the face of Jesus on a rectangle of cloth was the first icon. The remaining two flags have arms and hands extending from the clouds (it is unclear if the arms belong to God or to an angel). On the flag of Kirov Oblast, the arm holds a bow and arrow; on Vologda Oblast's flag it holds an orb and sword.

Geographic Symbols

The diverse geography of Russia is represented on the flags of 12 federal subjects. Two flags include map-like representations of the territories. The flag of Sakhalin Oblast shows Sakhalin Island and the Kuril Islands against the background of the sea. On the flag of Stavropol Krai the arms show a map of the territory, including the line of the 45th parallel north and a white cross marking the location of the "City of the Cross".

Russia has many mountain ranges. One of the best known is the Caucasus—the dividing line between Europe and Asia. Two flags show the Caucasus Mountains: the flag of Kabardino-Balkaria shows Mount Elbrus, the highest mountain in Europe; Karachay-Cherkessia's flag shows a sunrise behind the same mountain. The flag of Voronezh Oblast also includes a mountain, but in a more stylized manner—it has a mountainside made of individual stones. Physical topography is also on the flag of Lipetsk, which shows five hills.

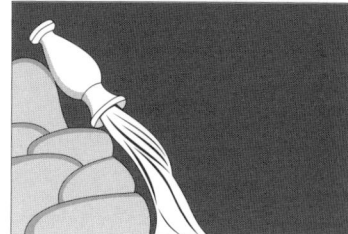

Figure 12: Mountains on the flags of (from top to bottom) Kabardino-Balkaria, Karachay-Cherkessia, and Voronezh Oblast.

Figure 13, Water on the flags of (clockwise, from top left) Amur Oblast, Ivanovo Oblast, Omsk Oblast, and Leningrad Oblast.

Water, of course, is important in every country. While on many flags the color blue represents the concept of water or specific bodies of water, on a number of flags water is a central part of the symbolism in the design. Two of the flags include wavy lines as the central emblem on their flags. Amur Oblast's flag has a narrow wavy white stripe atop a wider blue stripe, representing the Amur River. In contrast, a single blue wavy line runs vertically through the flag of Omsk Oblast, representing the Irtysh River. The Volga River inspired the three silver (or white) wavy lines running horizontally across both the arms and flag of Ivanovo Oblast. In addition, three federal subjects use scalloped waves of water as stripes along the bases of their flags (reminiscent of the old Soviet republic flags of Latvia and Estonia)—Leningrad Oblast, Magadan Oblast, and Ulyanovsk Oblast. On the flag of Voronezh Oblast, a stream of water flows out of a pitcher on a mountainside, symbolizing the Voronezh River.

Weapons, Tools, and Books

A variety of weapons are represented on a total of 14 flags. Adygea's flag has three arrows, while the flag of Kirov Oblast has a bow and arrow. Swords appear on six flags. The flag of Astrakhan Oblast bears a scimitar. The swords on the other five flags are being held by various figures on the flags. Tula Oblast's flag includes three sword blades, representing the region's role as a center of weapons manufacturing. Lances are on both flags that show St. George—those of Moscow Oblast and the city of Moscow. The bear on the flag of Yaroslavl Oblast holds a halberd, alluding to the legend about Yaroslav the Wise slaying a bear with his polearm at the site of the city. A gun carriage is on the arms shown on Smolensk Oblast's flag. In addition a small mortar from the city arms of Bryansk appears in the arms of Bryansk Oblast and on that oblast's flag.

Tools appear on 11 flags. The most prevalent is the hammer, shown on five different flags. Sickles are on two of those flags, as well as on a third flag. Picks (such as those used in mining) are on two flags, in both cases in combination with hammers. There is also a shovel on one flag—again, combined with a hammer. Other symbols in this category include a shuttle, a torch, a candlestick, a key, a pitcher, and two different types of anchor.

In addition, two flags include books as elements of the arms. The flag of Perm Krai depicts a Book of the Gospels, carried on the back of a bear. Oryol Oblast's arms include a secular book, representing the importance of literature.

Figure 14: Weapons on the flags of (from top to bottom) Adygea, Astrakhan Oblast, and Tula Oblast.

Celestial and Atmospheric Objects

Ten flags of the federal subjects include celestial objects—stars, the moon, and the sun. Interestingly, as pervasive a symbol as the star was in Soviet symbolism, only two of the flags include stars and in both cases the usage predates the Russian Revolution. The Republic of Adygea is using a flag with twelve 5-pointed yellow stars which was used by an independence movement as early as the 1830s.

 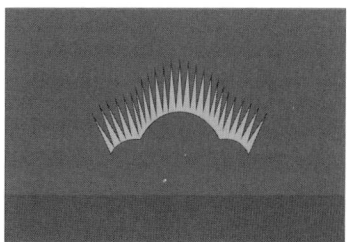

Figure 15: The white sun on the flag of (left) Sakha (Yakutia) and the Aurora Borealis on the flag of Murmansk Oblast.

Chuvashia's flag has three 8-pointed stars which have long been used in the culture of the region. Crescent moons appear on two flags—in the arms on the flag of Orenburg Oblast and as part of the *soyombo* symbol on the flag of Buryatia.

The sun appears on eight Russian subnational flags. A full solar disk is included in Buryatia's *soyombo*, as well as on the flag of Sakha (Yakutia). Karachay-Cherkessia's flag shows a sunrise behind the Caucasus Mountains. The other flags incorporate sun symbols (usually called "solar signs") used in the cultures of the different regions. Ingushetia's flag has a red solar sign that consists of a circle with three arms curving out from the circle. Khakassia's solar sign is more complex with a set of concentric circles and four triangular rays extending out from the perimeter. The flags of Mordovia and Udmurtia show the same basic symbol. On Udmurtia's flag it is shown as a single 8-pointed solar cross. In contrast, Mordovia's flag has this symbol split into four equal parts, shaped like an arrow's fletching and pointing inward. Mari El's flag also has a type of solar symbol, although it is usually referred to as a Mari El Cross. For a more detailed discussion of solar signs, see the section on cultural symbols.

Four flags depict atmospheric phenomena. Two (Kirov Oblast and Vologda Oblast) have clouds, both presumably representing heaven. The flag of the Jewish Autonomous Oblast has a rainbow—like the clouds, a religious symbol. Murmansk Oblast's flag has a natural phenomenon unique to the northern regions of the world—the *Aurora Borealis* or Northern Lights.

Structures and Transportation

Various man-made structures are shown on flags of the federal subjects. Fortresses appear in the arms on the flags of Krasnodar Krai, Stavropol Krai, and Oryol Oblast. A fortress is also the major element on the flag of Kaliningrad Oblast. In addition, other types of structures are evident on various flags, mostly as elements of coats of arms—Altai Krai has a blast furnace on its arms, a wall is in the arms of Leningrad Oblast, Magadan Oblast's arms have a hydroelectric dam, and there is a column on the arms of Ulyanovsk Oblast. Another large structure is on the flag of Volgograd Oblast. This immense statue is 85 meters (279 feet) tall and weighs 7,900 tons. The monument was erected in Volgograd (then called Stalingrad) to recognize the city's "Hero City" status from the Battle of Stalingrad during World War II. Perhaps the most unique structures on any of the flags, however, are the burial mounds on the flag of Kurgan Oblast. The word for a burial mound of this type is *kurgan*, the source of the oblast's name.

Transportation symbols appear on eight subnational flags of Russia. Three of those flags have transport animals—two with saddled horses (Moscow Oblast and the city of Moscow) and a pack camel (on the flag of Chelyabinsk Oblast). Nautical transportation is represented on three flags. Kostroma Oblast has an imperial galleon, while the flags of Leningrad Oblast and the city of St. Petersburg both have anchors. Aviation is represented by the airplane on the arms and flag of Magadan Oblast. In addition, the Trans-Siberian Railway is symbolized by a thin black/white/black line below the arms on Novosibirsk Oblast's flag.

Soviet Legacies

Obviously, the Soviet period has left a tremendous legacy on Russia, a legacy reflected on many flags of the federal subjects. Looking back on the history of the Soviet Union, one event appears to have had the most impact on the flags—the conflict which the Soviets called the Great Patriotic War. World War II had a tragic impact on the people and territories of the USSR and Soviet Russia. It is estimated that the Soviet Union suffered about 10.6 million military deaths and lost 14-17 million civilians as a result of the Nazi invasion. Even today, the war is a symbol of great patriotism and sacrifice for the homeland. As a result of their heroism during World War II, a number of regions received the Order of Lenin. The ribbon of this medal—red with two narrow yellow stripes at the edges—appears in the arms on five flags (Krasnodar Krai, Krasnoyarsk Krai, Bryansk Oblast, Kemerovo Oblast, and Tambov Oblast). It also influenced the field of the flag of Smolensk Oblast. Bryansk Oblast's arms also include a second ribbon—that of the Partisans of the Patriotic War. Another legacy from World War II is the sculpture on the flag of Volgograd Oblast. This statue is a monument to the Soviet victory in the Battle of Stalingrad (the name of the city at the time).

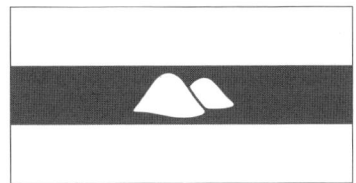

Figure 16: Structures from the flags of (from top to bottom) Kaliningrad Oblast (a fortress), Altai Krai (a blast furnace), and Kurgan Oblast (burial mounds).

Figure 17. The Soviet-inspired designs of (from top to bottom) Bryansk Oblast, Vladimir Oblast, and Altai Krai.

Two flags have retained the hammer and sickle symbols prevalent on flags during the Soviet period. They are Bryansk Oblast and Vladimir Oblast. Other flags reflect the Soviet legacy through designs which look quite similar to the symbols used in Soviet arms and flags. For example, while the arms on Altai Krai's flag include symbols that predate the Soviet Union, the overall presentation of the arms and the shaft of grain near the hoist retain a certain Soviet style. The arms on the flag of Magadan Oblast also include symbols of progress of the type popular in the Soviet Union— an airplane and a hydroelectric dam.

There are also flags which at first glance might appear to use Soviet symbols, but are actually based on arms which predate the USSR. One is the flag of Tula Oblast with its array of blades and hammers. This arrangement is based upon the city arms of Tula which date to 1778. The sickle held by the lion on the arms of Krasnoyarsk Krai is pre-Soviet in origin, appearing in the city arms of Krasnoyarsk in 1851.[17]

Cultural Symbols

The cultural diversity of the federal subjects is evident in the wide variety of cultural symbols on their flags. Many of the republics use distinctive symbols from the cultures of their people. The *kurai* flower on Bashkortostan's flag and the *soyombo* on that of Buryatia are important cultural symbols in those regions.

Various solar signs on the flags of Ingushetia, Khakassia, Mordovia, and Udmurtia are also cultural symbols. A similar symbol, sometimes called a solar sign but usually referred to as a Mari El cross, is on the flag of Mari El. Solar signs are commonly described not only as symbols of the sun, but also as representing

---

17. "Gerb goroda Tula", *Geral'dika.ru*, http://geraldika.ru/symbols/1470, accessed 27 August 2008; "Gerb goroda Krasnoiarsk (1851 g.)", *Geral'dika.ru*, http://geraldika.ru/symbols/451, accessed 27 August 2008.

Figure 18. Cultural symbols on the flags of (left) Bashkortostan and Buryatia.

fire, fertility, and renewal of life. At one time, they were believed to have protective powers and were a common motif in clothing decorations. Another flag with distinctive cultural symbols is that of Chuvashia, which includes a stylized Tree of Life and three 8-pointed stars—all traditional symbols in the Chuvash culture. All of these patterns suggest motifs that might be found in embroidery or other cultural decorations of the regions. Chechnya's flag includes a repeating Chechen national ornament at the hoist, a pattern that could be drawn from embroidery or rug designs.[18]

Another symbol used in cultural decorations is on the flag of Tyumen Oblast, as well as on the flags of three autonomous okrugs. On the oblast's flag are three stylized crowns described as traditional ornaments of the people. They appear to be made of reindeer antlers. This same symbol is the principal emblem on the flag of Khanty-Mansi Autonomous Okrug, which is part of the territory of Tyumen Oblast. On the flags of Yamalo-Nenets Autonomous Okrug (also territorially part of Tyumen Oblast) and Nenets Autonomous Okrug the emblem is repeated across the length of the flags and more closely resembles the patterns on traditional clothing.[19]

---

18. "Embroidery", in Pronin and Pronin, *Russian Folk Arts*, p. 142-158; Nina T. Klimova, *Folk Embroidery of the USSR* (New York: Van Nostrand Reinhold Co., 1981), p. 13-15; Muzei narodnogo iskusstva, *Izobrazitel'nye motivy v russkoi narodnoi vyshivke* (Moskva: Sovetskaia Rossiia, 1990); Finno-ugorskii kul'turnyi tsentr Rossiiskoi Federatsii, "Mariitsy: Ornament", *Informatsionnyi tsentr "Finnougoriia"*, http://www.finnougoria.ru/community/folk/12/detail.php?IBLOCK_ID=46&SECTION_ID=350&ELEMENT_ID=2337, accessed 30 July 2008; Mari El cross embroidery image is based upon an image found on the website of the Finno-ugorskii kul'turnyi tsentr Rossiiskoi Federatsii, http://www.finnougoria.ru/upload/iblock/68f/smgizplb.gif, accessed 30 July 2008.

19. Finno-ugorskii kul'turnyi tsentr Rossiiskoi Federatsii, "Nenetsy: Dekorativnoe tvorchesvo", *Informatsionnyi tsentr "Finnougoriia"*, http://www.finnougoria.ru/community/folk/15/detail.php?IBLOCK_ID=46&SECTION_ID=353&ELEMENT_ID=2398, accessed 30 July 2008; Finno-ugorskii kul'turnyi tsentr Rossiiskoi Federatsii, "Komi-Permiaki: Ornament", *Informatsionnyi tsentr "Finnougoriia"*, http://www.finnougoria.ru/community/folk/9/detail.php?IBLOCK_ID=46&SECTION_ID=347&ELEMENT_ID=2277, accessed 30 July 2008.

30 *Russian Regional Flags*

Figure 19. The Tree of Life symbol on Chuvashia's flag, the Chechen national ornament on Chechnya's flag, and a variety of solar signs on the flags of Mordovia, Udmurtia, Mari El, Ingushetia, and Khakassia.

Figure 20. Variation of the Mari El Cross as an embroidery motif.

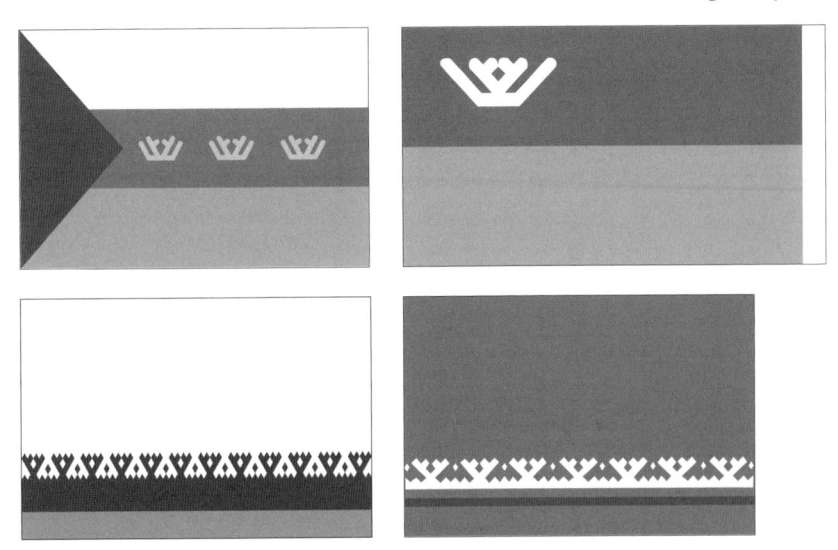

Figure 21. The crowns and reindeer antler ornaments of (clockwise, from top left) Tyumen Oblast, Khanty-Mansi Autonomous Okrug, Yamalo-Nenets Autonomous Okrug, and Nenets Autonomous Okrug.

Summary

Currently 81 federal subjects of Russia—all but two—have their own flags. The designs are colorful and distinctive. Striped designs (72%) outnumber the flags with solid fields (22%). However, only a small number of flags rely solely upon stripes for their symbolism. The majority of designs are more complex and unique. Each flag represents a different region, uses different colors, and incorporates different symbols. While many flags have similar designs, no one pattern dominates. As a result, the flags of the federal subjects are a colorful collection of unique symbols. One clear trend is the heraldic nature of the flags—81% of the flags are based in some way upon the regional coats of arms.

Russian sources are usually careful to stress that the Russian Federation *consists of* 83 federal subjects, rather than to say that it is *divided into* 83 federal subjects. The phraseology may seem like semantics, but it is an important distinction for the Russians. Each federal subject is considered an integral, indivisible part of the Russian Federation. In the designs of their flags and the symbolism assigned to them, the majority of the federal subjects stress their role as a part of the greater whole. They do so through the use of the national colors and through the use of symbols which demonstrate their unity with Russia. In addition, most federal subjects have adopted the official 2:3 proportions of the national flag. It seems that the lessons of Russian history have taught that the whole is stronger than any individual territory.

While modern Russia still faces many challenges, it seems to be coming to terms with its diversity and with its past. Across the flags of the federal subjects one can find the symbols of a range of peoples, each with their own unique culture. Four major world religions are symbolized in flags of the federal subjects. It is interesting to see the wide variety of cultural symbols drawn from the traditions of the many peoples who live in the country.

The story of Russian history is told in many of the flags—the time of the tsars and the Russian Empire, the period of the Soviet Union, the trauma of invasion and the glory of victory, and the contrast of ancient traditions and industrial development. A consistent theme across the designs is the willingness of the people to defend their homeland.

It is also interesting to see how the flag designs illustrate the geographic diversity and the immense size of the Russian Federation. The shores of the Baltic Sea and the Pacific coast, the mountains of the Caucasus, the sunny regions in the south, the snowy regions of the north, and the vastness of Siberia—all are represented on the flags. A number of the flags depict water in their designs, and even more assign water-related symbolism to the color blue in their flags. All of the major rivers of the Russian Federation, and the coastlines with a variety of seas and oceans, are represented. A wide variety of wildlife appears on the flags, including eagles, partridges, fish, bees, camels, bears, martens, sables, and Siberian tigers—all demonstrating the diverse fauna of the country.

As a result of the wide variety of designs and the broad range of symbolism used, a study of the flag designs of the federal subjects tells a great deal about the regions of Russia, and about the Russian Federation as a whole, and each flag has a story to tell.

Flag Descriptions: Federal Subjects

Names of the federal subjects are first given in the most common English-language version, followed by the official name in Russian and a transliteration of that name into Latin characters. Republics are typically called just by their short names, but other federal subjects will be called by their full names to avoid confusion with cities of the same names.

Descriptions are listed alphabetically by the English name of the subject. In addition to information about the flag, each entry identifies the subject's federal district, the name of the capital city or administrative center, and the population as of 1 January 2009.

Federal Districts of the Russian Federation (Source: Wikipedia Commons).

1. Central Federal District
2. Southern Federal District
3. Northwestern Federal District
4. Far Eastern Federal District
5. Siberian Federal District
6. Urals Federal District
7. Volga Federal District

Registration of Flags and Arms

The heraldic authority for the Russian Federation is the Heraldic Council, created by a presidential decree in 1996. It serves as an advisory body on heraldic issues and as an authority for the registration of official symbols in the Russian Federation. Registration of federal subjects' symbols is optional and does not affect their legal status. However, the registration process creates a uniform system of heraldry in the Russian Federation, ensures that symbols conform to heraldic standards, and applies federal protection to registered territorial symbols. While many federal subjects have registered their flags and arms with the Council, a number remain unregistered, either because they do not conform to heraldic standards or because the registration process has yet to be completed.[20]

---

20. "O Geral'dicheskom Sovete pri Presidente RF", *Geral'dika.ru*, http://sovet.geraldika.ru/part/10, accessed 17 October 2009; "Gosudarstvennyi geral'dicheskii registr Rossiiskoi Federatsii, http://www.rossimvolika.ru/gerald_sovet/gerald_reg/, accessed 17 October 2009.

Adygea, Republic of
Республика Адыгея / Respublika Adygeia

Year Adopted: 1992   **Proportions:** 1:2
Designer: O. L. Pletneva

Federal District: Southern
Capital: Maykop
Population: 442,775

The flag of Adygea consists of a green field with twelve 5-pointed stars and three crossed arrows, all in yellow. Nine stars form an arch that begins and ends two-thirds down from the top of the flag. The remaining three stars form a straight line just below the top of the arch. All stars point upwards. Below the stars are the three crossed arrows with their tips pointing upward. The stars represent the 12 Adyghe tribes and the crossing of the arrows indicates the unity of the tribes. Green is the color of Islam and also represents the eternity of life, hope, plenty, freedom, and the natural features of the republic. A similar flag was first used in the 1830s by those seeking independence of Cherkessia from Russia. A similar design was also used during World War II by the pro-German North Caucasian League.

Sources: Respublika Adygeia, "Simvolika", http://www.adygheya.ru/info/symbolism/index.shtml, accessed 13 June 2008; "Flag Respubliki Adygeia", *Geral'dika.ru*, http://geraldika.ru/symbols/97, accessed 17 June 2008; "Respublika Adygeia", *Vexillographia: Flagi Rossii*, http://www.vexillographia.ru/russia/subjects/adygeja.htm, accessed 1 August 2008; Igor' Vladimirovich Borisov and Elena Nikolaevna Kozina, *Geral'dika Rossii* (Moskva: AST/Astrel', 2006), p. 24; Viktor Nikolaevich Saprykov, *Gosudarstvennaia simvolika regionov Rossii* (Moskva: Parad, 2004), p. 11; Saprykov, (2006), p. 8; F. I. Sharkov, *Vetry peremen: flagi i gerby respublik Rossii / Winds of Change: Flags and Coats of Arms of the Russian Repub-*

lics, (Shupashkar (Cheboksary): Chuvashiia, 1992), p.13, 107, [195], [202]; Igor' Stanislavovich Smetannikov, *Gerby i flagi sub"ektov Rossiiskoi Federatsii* (Moskva: Kompaniia Ritm Esteit, 2003), p. 18; Vladimir Solov'ëv, *Simvolika Rossii* (Moscow: Profizda, 2004), p. 82-83; "Adygeya (Russia)", *FOTW Flags of the World*, http://www.crwflags.com/FOTW/flags/ru-01.html, accessed 27 June 2008.

Altai Krai
Алтайский край / Altaiskii krai

Year Adopted: 2000 **Proportions:** 1:2
Designer: unknown

Federal District: Siberian
Administrative Center: Barnaul
Population: 2,496,776

The flag of Altai Krai is red with a blue stripe at the hoist. In the blue stripe is a stylized ear of grain symbolizing agriculture. Centered on the flag are the arms of the krai. In the upper portion of the arms is the image of an 18th-century blast furnace. Below it is a large vessel, the "Tsarina of vases"—a large jasper vase now housed in the State Hermitage Museum. A wreath of grain wrapped in a blue ribbon encircles the shield. The colors of the flag come from the flag of the Russian SFSR, within which the territory of Altai Krai was organized in 1937. These colors also symbolize the krai's role as a federal subject of the Russian Federation.

Sources: Altaiskii krai, "Flag Altaiskogo kraia", http://www.altairegion22.ru/rus/territory/flag/, accessed 14 June 2008; "Flag Altaiskogo kraia", *Geral'dika.ru*, http://geraldika.ru/symbols/434, accessed 18 June 2008; "Altaiskii krai", *Vexillographia: Flagi Rossii*, http://www.vexillographia.ru/russia/subjects/altaj.htm, accessed 1 August 2008; Borisov and Kozina, p. 70; Saprykov (2004), p. 31; Saprykov (2006), p. 29; Smetannikov, p. 39; Solov'ëv, p. 164-165; "Altay Territory (Russia)", *FOTW Flags of the World*, http://www.crwflags.com/FOTW/flags/ru-22.html, accessed 27 June 2008.

Altai Republic
Республика Алтай / Respublika Altai

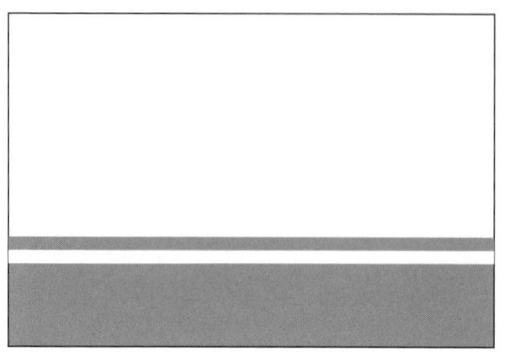

Year Adopted: 1993   **Proportions:** 2:3; changed from 1:2 in 1996
Designer: Vladimir Petrovich Chukuev

Federal District: Siberian
Capital: Gorno-Altaysk
Population: 209,207

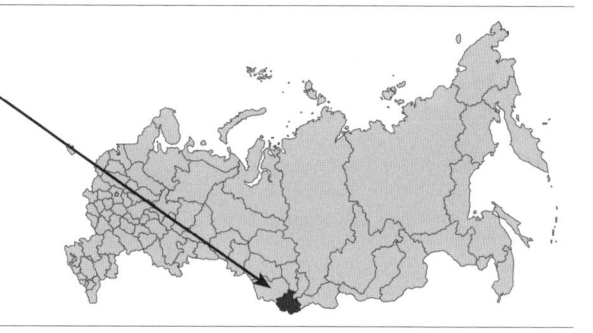

Altai's flag has a white field with horizontal stripes of light blue, white, and light blue running across the base. The upper two stripes are 1/25 the width of the flag; the lower stripe is 1/4 the width of the flag. White and blue come from the colors of the Russian Federation and emphasize the republic's role as a federal subject. The color white represents eternity, aspiration to revival, love, and the consent of the people. Blue symbolizes the cleanliness of the sky, the mountains, the rivers, and the lakes of Altai.

Sources: Respublika Altai, "Gosudarstvennii Flag Respubliki Altai", http://www.altai-republic.com/modules.php?op=m odload&name=Sections&file=index&req=viewarticle&artid=17&page=1, accessed 13 June 2008; "Flag Respubliki Altai", *Geral'dika.ru*, http://geraldika.ru/symbols/105, accessed 17 June 2008; "Respublika Altai", *Vexillographia: Flagi Rossii*, http://www.vexillographia.ru/russia/subjects/altaj_g.htm, accessed 1 August 2008; Borisov and Kozina, p. 26; Saprykov (2004), p. 12; Saprykov (2006), p. 9; Sharkov, p. 14-17, 108-111; Smetannikov, p. 19; Solov'ëv, p. 156-157; "Altay (Russia)", *FOTW Flags of the World*, http://www.crwflags.com/FOTW/flags/ru-04.html, accessed 27 June 2008.

Amur Oblast
Амурская область / Amurskaia oblast'

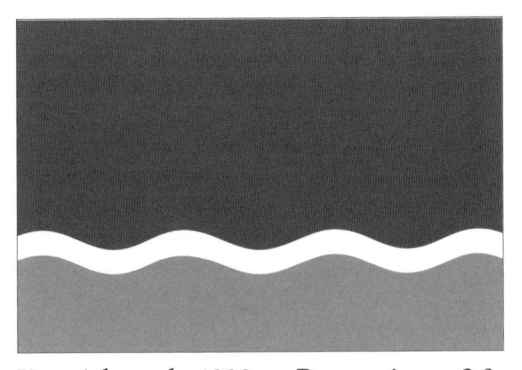

Year Adopted: 1999   **Proportions:** 2:3
Designer: unknown

Federal District: Far Eastern
Administrative Center: Blagoveshchensk
Population: 864,458

The flag of Amur Oblast has horizontal stripes—red over blue, divided by a wavy white line. The proportions of the stripes at the hoist are 8:1:3. Red symbolizes the rich history of Priamurye (another name for the region) and centuries of defending the region, as well as the successes of economic development. The white wave and the blue stripe represent the Amur River. On the arms, the stripes are green.

Sources: Amurskaia oblast', "Simvolika", http://www.amurobl.ru/index.php?m=24596&r=4, accessed 14 June 2008; "Flag Amurskoi oblasti", *Geral'dika.ru*, http://geraldika.ru/symbols/488, accessed 19 June 2008; "Amurskaia oblast'", *Vexillographia: Flagi Rossii*, http://www.vexillographia.ru/russia/subjects/amurska.htm, accessed 1 August 2008; Borisov and Kozina, p. 94; Saprykov (2004), p. 37; Saprykov (2006), p. 35; Smetannikov, p. 45; Solov'ëv, p. 196-197; "Amur Region (Russia)", *FOTW Flags of the World*, http://www.crwflags.com/FOTW/flags/ru-amu.html, accessed 27 June 2008.

Arkhangelsk Oblast
Архангельская область / Arkhangel'skaia oblast'

Year Adopted: 2009   **Proportions:** 2:3
Designer: unknown

Federal District: Northwestern
Administrative Center: Arkhangelsk
Population: 1,262,036

The flag of Arkhangelsk Oblast recalls the *Andreevskii* flag used by the Russian navy. A St. Andrew's cross in azure (blue/light blue) appears on a white field. Centered on the cross are the arms of the region. The blue derives from the armor of the Archangel Michael, namesake of the oblast and a symbol of good. In the arms, Michael vanquishes a demon, representing evil. He also represents the defenders of Russia and their strength. The arms and flag also reflect the role of Arkhangelsk as a naval port important to the defense of Russia.

Sources: Administratsiia Arkhangel'skoi oblasti, "Y Arkhangel'skoi oblasti poiavilsia svoi flag", http://www.dvinaland.ru/prcenter/release/8615/ and "Simvolika", http://www.dvinaland.ru/region/symbols.html, accessed 29 September 2009; "Flag Arkhangel'skoi oblasti", *Geral'dika.ru*, http://geraldika.ru/symbols/24295, accessed 29 September 2009; "Gerb Arkhangel'skoi oblasti", *Geral'dika.ru*, http://geraldika.ru/symbols/16551, accessed 29 September 2009; "Arkhangel'skaia oblast'", *Vexillographia: Flagi Rossii*, http://www.vexillographia.ru/russia/subjects/arhangel.htm, accessed 29 September 2009.

Astrakhan Oblast
Астраханская область / Astrakhanskaia oblast'

Year Adopted: 2001   **Proportions:** 2:3
Designer: N. Ukolov

Federal District: Southern
Administrative Center: Astrakhan
Population: 1,005,241

Astrakhan Oblast's flag is blue with two symbols—a crown above a scimitar. Blue symbolizes the location of the oblast at the upper region of the Volga River. The crown is in the style of that made for Mikhail Fedorovich, the first ruler of the Romanov Dynasty. It is gold with a green lining and has five metal arches, decorated with pearls and gems, which curve to the top of the crown where they join and are topped with an orb and cross. The crown is approximately 1/4 the length of the flag. Below the crown, the sword has a gold handle and a silver blade pointing toward the hoist. It is approximately 2/3 the length of the flag. The eastern-style sword symbolizes the direction from which the enemies of Russia came, and its placement with the crown represents centuries of unity with Russia and defense of the crown.

Sources: Astrakhanskaia oblast', "Flag Astrakhanskoi oblasti", http://www.astrobl.ru/Default.aspx?id=9&item=20, accessed 14 June 2008 "Flag Astrakhanskoi oblasti", *Geral'dika.ru*, http://geraldika.ru/symbols/129, accessed 19 June 2008; "Astrakhanskaia oblast'", *Vexillographia: Flagi Rossii*, http://www.vexillographia.ru/russia/subjects/astrakan.htm, accessed 1 August 2008; Borisov and Kozina, p. 101; Saprykov (2004), p. 38; Saprykov (2006), p. 37; Smetannikov, p. 47; Solov'ëv, p. 102-103 "Astrakhan Region (Russia)", *FOTW Flags of the World*, http://www.crwflags.com/FOTW/flags/ru-ast.html, accessed 27 June 2008.

Bashkortostan, Republic of
Республика Башкортостан / Respublika Bashkortostan

Year Adopted: 1992   **Proportions:** 2:3; changed from 1:2 in 2003.
Designers: Ol'ga Evgen'evna Asabina and Ural Temirbulatovich Masalimov

Federal District: Volga
Capital: Ufa
Population: 4,057,292

The flag of Bashkortostan has equal horizontal stripes of blue, white, and green. In the center of the white stripe is a stylized *kurai* flower with 7 petals in yellow, enclosed within a yellow circle. Its diameter is 1/4 of the width of the flag. The *kurai* flower is a symbol of friendship and the petals represent the unity of different ethnicities living in the republic. Green represents freedom and the eternity of life; white symbolizes the peaceful disposition, openness, and readiness for mutual cooperation of the people of Bashkortostan; and blue represents the clarity, virtue, and purity of their thoughts. The colors of the stripes recall a flag designed by Bashkir nationalist Akhmetzaki Akhmetshakhovich Valigov in 1917. When the flag was finally adopted, the order of the colors was changed and the *kurai* flower emblem added. The emblem was designed by Nil Khabibylin.

Sources: Respublika Bashkortostan, "Gosudarstvennaia Simvolika," http://www.bashkortostan.ru/index.cfm?id=803, accessed 13 June 2008; "Flag Respubliki Bashkortostan", *Geral'dika.ru*, http://geraldika.ru/symbols/110, accessed 17 June 2008; "Respublika Bashkortostan", *Vexillographia: Flagi Rossii*, http://www.vexillographia.ru/russia/subjects/baskiria.htm, accessed 1 August 2008; Borisov and Kozina, p. 26-27; Saprykov (2004), p. 13; Saprykov (2006), p. 10; Sharkov, p. 18-25, 112-118; Smetannikov, p. 20; Solov'ëv, p. 110-111; "Bashkiria (Russia)", *FOTW Flags of the World*, http://www.crwflags.com/FOTW/flags/ru-02.html, accessed 27 June 2008.

Belgorod Oblast
Белгородская область / Belgorodskaia oblast'

Year Adopted: 2000 **Proportions:** 2:3
Designers: V. M. Pal'val', A. V. Kulabukhov, V. P. Legeza, and A. V. Riabchikov

Federal District: Central
Administrative Center: Belgorod
Population: 1,525,083

The flag of Belgorod Oblast has a blue cross dividing the flag into four panels: white at upper hoist, green at upper fly, red at lower hoist, and black at lower fly. The width of cross is roughly 1/8 the width of the flag. Centered in the white panel are the arms of the region which feature a black-and-white eagle in flight above a resting lion in gold on a base of green. White symbolizes milk and sugar as well as chalk deposits and manufacturing. Green represents the abundance and fertility of the land, fields, and forests. Red recalls the blood spilled by the defenders of the fatherland in the region during the 16th through 20th centuries. Black is for the riches of the ground, its *chernozëm* (a rich black topsoil found in the central part of European Russia), and the resources under the ground. The blue of the cross matches the field of the arms. Symbols in the arms represent both Sweden (the lion, from the royal standard of Sweden's King Charles XII) and Russia (the eagle, inspired by the standard of Tsar Peter I).

Sources: "Flag Belgorodskoi oblasti" *Geral'dika.ru*, http://geraldika.ru/symbols/596, accessed 19 June 2008; "Belgorodskaia oblast'", *Vexillographia: Flagi Rossii*, http://www.vexillographia.ru/russia/subjects/belgorod.htm, accessed 1 August 2008; Borisov and Kozina, p. 104; Saprykov (2004), p. 39; Saprykov (2006), p. 38; Smetannikov, p. 48; Solov'ëv, p. 20-21 "Belgorod Region (Russia)", *FOTW Flags of the World*, http://www.crwflags.com/FOTW/flags/ru-31.html, accessed 27 June 2008.

Bryansk Oblast
Брянская область / Brianskaia oblast'

Year Adopted: 1998 **Proportions:** 2:3
Designer: unknown

Federal District: Central
Administrative Center: Bryansk
Population: 1,299,690

Bryansk Oblast has a red flag with the arms of the oblast in the center, just over half the length of the flag. Red is a traditional color for symbols of the oblast. It is the color of the arms of the city of Bryansk and symbolizes the era when the oblast was established. The prominent symbol on the arms is a spruce tree in gold—a symbol of the forests in the oblast. Centered on the tree are the arms of the city of Bryansk with a small mortar. The blue shield of the oblast's arms is topped with a hammer and sickle. These symbols represent the indestructible union of workers and peasants, and also recognize that the territory was organized by Soviet authorities.

Sources: Brianskaia oblast', "O simvolakh Brianskoi oblasti", http://www.bryanskobl.ru/region/law/view.php?type=0&id=1409, accessed 14 June 2008; "Flag Brianskoi oblasti", *Geral'dika.ru*, http://geraldika.ru/symbols/649, accessed 19 June 2008; "Brianskaia oblast'", *Vexillographia: Flagi Rossii*, http://www.vexillographia.ru/russia/subjects/bryansk.htm, accessed 1 August 2008; Borisov and Kozina, p. 108; Saprykov (2004), p. 40; Saprykov (2006), p. 39; Smetannikov, p. 49; Solov'ëv, p. 22-23 "Bryansk Region (Russia)", *FOTW Flags of the World*, http://www.crwflags.com/FOTW/flags/ru-bry.html, accessed 27 June 2008.

Buryatia (Buryat Republic)
Республика Бурятия / Respublika Buriatiia

Year Adopted: 1992   **Proportions:** 1:2
Designers: N. Batuev, V. Abaev, and S. Kalmykov

Federal District: Siberian
Capital: Ulan-Ude
Population: 960,742

    Buryatia's flag has three horizontal stripes: blue over white over yellow in proportions of 2:1:1. In the upper stripe, 1/4 the distance from the hoist, is a yellow *soyombo*—the traditional symbol of Buryatia. This symbol is similar to that used in Mongolia, except that it comprises only three elements: a 3-tongued flame, the sun, and a crescent moon. The flame represents warmth, life, light, revival, well-being, and the hearth. It is also a symbol of cleanliness and the keeper of the home. In addition, the three tongues of the flame symbolize the past, the present, and the future; combined they represent the concepts of continuity and succession. Below the flame is the sun, which symbolizes the source of life, vitality, wealth, and abundance. In the culture of the region, as in much of Asia, the moon is revered as the "master of the night" and is the basis of the local calendar. Blue is the national color of Buryatia and represents the historical roots and cultural connections of the people. It also represents inviolability and loyalty. White symbolizes lofty moral beginnings, happiness, tranquility, well-being, peace, unity, and integrity. Combined, these two colors stand for the status of Buryatia as part of the Russian Federation. Yellow symbolizes spiritual beginnings and is the traditional color of Lamaism and Buddhism. It also represents mercy, harmony of a person and nature, and spiritual perfection.

Sources: Respublika Buriatiia, "Gosudarstvennaia Simvolika," http://egov-buryatia.ru/index.php?id=1570, accessed 13 June 2008; "Flag Respubliki Buryatiia", *Geral'dika.ru*, http://geraldika.ru/symbols/132, accessed 17 June 2008; "Buriatiia", *Vexillographia: Flagi Rossii*, http://www.vexillographia.ru/russia/subjects/buriat.htm, accessed 1 August 2008; Borisov and Kozina, p. 30; Saprykov (2004), p. 14; Saprykov (2006), p. 11; Sharkov, p. 26-28; 119-121; Smetannikov, p. 21; Solov'ëv, p. 158-159; "Buriatia (Russia)", *FOTW Flags of the World*, http://www.crwflags.com/FOTW/flags/ru-bu.html, accessed 27 June 2008.

Chechnya (Chechen Republic)
Чеченская Республика / Chechenskaia Respublika

Year Adopted: 2004 **Proportions:** 2:3
Designer: unknown

Federal District: Southern
Capital: Grozny
Population: 1,238,452

At the hoist of Chechnya's flag is a vertical white stripe whose width is approximately 1/8 the length of the flag. It is decorated with a Chechen national ornament in yellow, symbolizing the ancient culture of the Chechen people. The rest of the flag comprises three horizontal stripes of green, white, and red in proportions of approximately 4:1:3. Green in the flag represents Islam, the principal religion of the region.

Sources: Chechenskaia Respublika, "Flag Chechenskoi Respubliki", http://chechnya.gov.ru/page.php?r=74, accessed 14 June 2008 "Flag Chechenskoi Respubliki", *Geral'dika.ru*, http://geraldika.ru/symbols/6570, accessed 17 June 2008; "Flag Chechni (1999 g.)", *Geral'dika.ru*, http://geraldika.ru/symbols/410, accessed 10 August 2008; "Chechenskaia Respublika", *Vexillographia: Flagi Rossii*, http://www.vexillographia.ru/russia/subjects/chechnya.htm, accessed 1 August 2008; Borisov and Kozina, p. 62; Saprykov (2006), p. 27; Sharkov, p. 89, 182, [201], [208]; Smetannikov, p. 37; Solov'ëv, p. 96-97; "Chechenia (Russia)", *FOTW Flags of the World*, http://www.crwflags.com/FOTW/flags/ru-ce.html, accessed 27 June 2008.

Chelyabinsk Oblast
Челябинская область / Cheliabinskaia oblast'

Year Adopted: 2001   **Proportions:** 2:3
Designers: K. F. Mochënov, R. I. Malanichev, S. A. Isaev, and G. A. Tunik

Federal District: Urals
Administrative Center: Chelyabinsk
Population: 3,508,733

Chelyabinsk Oblast's flag has three horizontal stripes—red over yellow over red in proportions of 4:1:1. Centered in the flag on the top two stripes is a white Bactrian (two-humped) camel loaded with cargo, nearly two-thirds the height of the hoist. Red is the color of life, mercy, and love; it also symbolizes courage, strength, fire, feelings, beauty, and health. In addition, it is a symbol of industrial development. Yellow represents the Ural Mountains which connect Europe and Asia, as well as their beauty, greatness, and mineral resources. White is a symbol of nobility, purity, justice, and magnanimity. The camel is a hardy and noble animal which inspires respect. It symbolizes wisdom, longevity, memory, fidelity, and patience.

Sources: "Flag Cheliabinskoi oblasti", *Geral'dika.ru*, http://geraldika.ru/symbols/90, accessed 20 June 2008; "Cheliabinskaia oblast'", *Vexillographia: Flagi Rossii*, http://www.vexillographia.ru/russia/subjects/celabins.htm, accessed 1 August 2008; Borisov and Kozina, p. 330; Saprykov (2004), p. 80; Saprykov (2006), p. 80; Smetannikov, p. 91; Solov'ëv, p. 148-149; "Chelyabinsk Region (Russia)", *FOTW Flags of the World*, http://www.crwflags.com/FOTW/flags/ru-74.html, accessed 27 June 2008.

Chukotka Autonomous Okrug
Чукотский автономный округ / Chukotskii avtonomnyi okrug

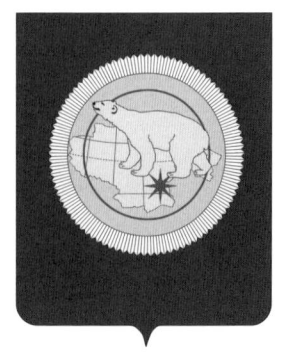

Year Adopted: 1994   **Proportions:** 2:3; changed from 1:2 in 1997
Designer: A. A. Nikolaeva

Federal District: Far Eastern
Administrative Center: Anadyr
Population: 49,520

The flag of Chukotka Autonomous Okrug (or Chukchi A.O.) is blue with a white equilateral triangle at the hoist. Centered in the triangle is a yellow disk, with a circular version of the Russian tricolor in its center. The triangle represents a figurative image of the territory. Its size on the flag symbolizes the huge territory and infinite open space in the region. White is for the Arctic, snowy open spaces, purity, and the fragility of the land. Together, blue and white represent the polar nights of winter and the white nights of summer. Blue is the color of the sea and the two sides of the triangle bordering the blue field represent the territory projecting into the Arctic and Pacific Oceans. The blue also symbolizes the many reservoirs in the territory. The yellow disk is reminiscent of how the sun rises on the Chukchi Peninsula (at the far eastern coast of Russia). It is also reminiscent of a *yarar*—a musical instrument of the Chukchi people. Yellow also represents gold and gold mining.

Sources: "Flag Chukotskogo avtonomnogo okruga", *Geral'dika.ru*, http://geraldika.ru/symbols/527, accessed 18 June 2008; "Chukotskii avtonomnyi okrug", *Vexillographia: Flagi Rossii*, http://www.vexillographia.ru/russia/subjects/chukotka.htm, accessed 1 August 2008; Borisov and Kozina, p. 407; Saprykov (2004), p. 93; Saprykov (2006), p. 93; Smetannikov, p. 104; Solov'ëv, p. 208-209; "Chukotka (Russia)", *FOTW Flags of the World*, http://www.crwflags.com/FOTW/flags/ru-87.html, accessed 27 June 2008.

Chuvashia (Chuvash Republic)
Чувашская Республика / Chuvashskaia Respublika

Year Adopted: 1992   **Proportions:** 5:8
Designer: E. M. Iur'ev

Federal District: Volga
Capital: Cheboksary
Population: 1,279,359

  Chuvashia's flag has two colors. At the top the yellow field occupies approximately 3/4 of the flag. The official description calls the other color *purpurnyi (temno-krasnyi)*. Purpurnyi translates as "purple" or "crimson" and *temno-krasnyi* means "dark red", so it is probably best translated as "purplish-red". The bottom stripe is 1/4 of the width of the flag. Centered on the yellow field is a stylized Tree of Life, a symbol of revival. The trunk of the tree extends down to the red stripe in the center, and runs horizontally above the stripe toward both hoist and fly creating a yellow fimbriation between it and the bottom stripe. Above the Tree of Life are three 8-pointed stars, symbols frequently used in the Chuvash culture to represent beauty and perfection. Yellow symbolizes the sun which bestows life to all the Earth. Purplish-red represents the age-old aspirations of the people for freedom, allowing them to retain their traditions and distinctive character.

Sources: Chuvashskaia Respublika, "Flag", http://gov.cap.ru/hierarhy_cap.asp?page=./32/40/41, accessed 14 June 2008; "Flag Chuvashskoi Respubliki", *Geral'dika.ru*, http://geraldika.ru/symbols/421, accessed 17 June 2008; "Chuvashiia", *Vexillographia: Flagi Rossii*, http://www.vexillographia.ru/russia/subjects/chuvasia.htm, accessed 1 August 2008; Borisov and Kozina, p. 63; Saprykov (2004), p. 30; Saprykov (2006), p. 28; Sharkov, p. 90-100, 183-192; Smetannikov, p. 38; Solov'ëv, p. 120-121; "Chuvashia (Russia)", *FOTW Flags of the World*, http://www.crwflags.com/FOTW/flags/ru-cu.html, accessed 27 June 2008.

Dagestan, Republic of
Республика Дагестан / Respublika Dagestan

Year Adopted: 1994   **Proportions:** 2:3; changed from 1:2 in 2003
Designer: A. Sh. Muratchaev

Federal District: Southern
Capital: Makhachkala
Population: 2,711,679

The flag of Dagestan has equal horizontal stripes of green, light blue, and red. Green symbolizes life and the abundance of the land of Dagestan, and is also the color of Islam, the dominant religion in the region. Light blue is the color of the Caspian Sea, which borders the republic on the east. It also symbolizes beauty and the greatness of the people. Red represents democracy, the educational force of human reason during the creation of life, as well as the courage and bravery of the people in the mountainous region.

Sources: Respublika Dagestan, "Simvolika," http://www.e-dag.ru/republic/simvol.htm, accessed 13 June 2008; "Flag Respubliki Dagestan", *Geral'dika.ru*, http://geraldika.ru/symbols/142, accessed 17 June 2008; "Respublika Dagestan", *Vexillographia: Flagi Rossii*, http://www.vexillographia.ru/russia/subjects/dagestan.htm, accessed 1 August 2008; Borisov and Kozina, p. 32; Saprykov (2004), p. 15; Saprykov (2006), p. 12; Sharkov, p. 29-32, 122-125; Smetannikov, p. 22; Solov'ëv, p. 84-85; "Daghestan (Russia)", *FOTW Flags of the World*, http://www.crwflags.com/FOTW/flags/ru-da.html, accessed 27 June 2008.

Ingushetia, Republic of
Республика Ингушетия / Respublika Ingushetiia

Year Adopted: 1994 **Proportions:** 2:3
Designer: unknown

Federal District: Southern
Capital: Magas
Largest City: Nazran
Population: 508,090

Ingushetia's flag is white with green stripes at the top and bottom, each 1/6 the width of the flag. In the center is a red solar symbol—a circle with three beams whose curvature suggests a clockwise rotation. In some depictions the beams have bulbous tips. Green is for nature, abundance, and fertility of the land, and is the color of Islam, the dominant religion in the region. White represents purity of thoughts and actions. Red is for the centuries-old struggle of the Ingush people against injustice, and for the right to live on the land of their ancestors in peace and harmony with neighboring peoples. The solar sign represents the eternal movements of the Sun and the Earth, as well as the interconnection and infinity of all existance. The clockwise motion of the arms represents the revolution of the Earth and other planets around the Sun. This symbol signifies well-being and the endless development of the people toward prosperity.

Sources: Respublika Ingushetiia, "Gosudarstvennaya Simvolika," http://www.ingushetia.ru/about/simvol.shtml, accessed 13 June 2008; "Flag Respubliki Ingushetiia", *Geral'dika.ru*, http://geraldika.ru/symbols/148, accessed 17 June 2008; "Respublika Ingushetiia", *Vexillographia: Flagi Rossii*, http://www.vexillographia.ru/russia/subjects/inguset.htm, accessed 1 August 2008; Borisov and Kozina, p. 33-34; Saprykov (2004), p. 16; Saprykov (2006), p. 13; Sharkov, p. 33-37, 126-130; Smetannikov, p. 23; Solov'ëv, p. 86-87; "Ingushetia (Russia)", *FOTW Flags of the World*, http://www.crwflags.com/FOTW/flags/ru-06.html, accessed 27 June 2008.

Irkutsk Oblast
Иркутская область / Irkutskaia oblast'

Year Adopted: 1997 **Proportions:** 2:3
Designer: S. B. Demkov

Federal District: Siberian
Administrative Center: Irkutsk
Population: 2,505,577

The flag of Irkutsk Oblast consists of three vertical stripes—blue, white, and blue, in proportions of 1:2:1. Blue is for water—Lake Baikal, the Angara River, and other rivers in the area. White is for goodness, modesty, and the purity of the inhabitants' thoughts, as well as the snow-white winters of Siberia. Green in the stylized cedar branches symbolizes hope, joy, abundance, and the unique flora, fauna, and riches of the forest. In the center is a black *babr* with a sable in its mouth. *Babr* is an old Russian word meaning "tiger" (original shown at right). However, in 1857, when the arms of Irkutsk were redesigned in Moscow, the word was inadvertently changed to *bobr* ("beaver"). The animal was transformed into a strange carnivorous beaver-type creature that has been retained in the modern arms of the oblast.

Sources: Irkutskaia oblast', "O gerbe i flage Irkutskoi oblasti", http://www.govirk.ru/dokumenty/o%20gerbe%20i%20flage/default.aspx, accessed 14 June 2008; "Flag Irkutskoi oblasti", *Geral'dika.ru*, http://geraldika.ru/symbols/766, accessed 19 June 2008; "Irkutskaia oblast'", *Vexillographia: Flagi Rossii*, http://www.vexillographia.ru/russia/subjects/irkutsk.htm, accessed 1 August 2008; Borisov and Kozina, p. 138; Saprykov (2004), p. 46; Saprykov (2006), p. 45; Smetannikov, p. 55; Solov'ëv, p. 168-169; "Irkutsk Region (Russia)", *FOTW Flags of the World*, http://www.crwflags.com/FOTW/flags/ru-38.html, accessed 27 June 2008; "Babr", *Vikipediia*, no direct URL available, accessed 5 July 2008.

Ivanovo Oblast
Ивановская область / Ivanovskaia oblast'

Year Adopted: 1998   **Proportions:** 2:3
Designers: A. I. Zhestarev, A. A. Kornikov, S. A. Prikazchikov, V. P. Terent'ev, and V. Iu. Khalturin

Federal District: Central
Administrative Center: Ivanovo
Population: 1,073,071

Ivanovo Oblast's flag draws from the field of its arms. It consists of two equal vertical stripes—red at the hoist and azure/blue at the fly. Along the bottom are three narrow wavy horizontal lines in silver. Above the waves are the arms of the oblast with two vertical symbols in the center—a gold shuttle representing the textile industry and a silver torch symbolizing knowledge, education, and aspiration to progress. Red and blue are taken from the arms of Vladimir and Kostroma—provinces which once included the territory of modern Ivanova Oblast. The silver waves represent the Volga River. The arms are supported by a lion and an eagle, both in gold, and are topped with a crown.

Sources: Ivanovskaia oblast', "Simvolika" http://www.ivreg.ru/symbols/, accessed 14 June 2008; "Flag Ivanovskoi oblasti", *Geral'dika.ru*, http://geraldika.ru/symbols/748, accessed 19 June 2008; "Ivanovskaia oblast'", *Vexillographia: Flagi Rossii*, http://www.vexillographia.ru/russia/subjects/ivanovo.htm, accessed 1 August 2008; Borisov and Kozina, p. 134-135; Saprykov (2004), p. 45; Saprykov (2006), p. 44; Smetannikov, p. 54; Solov'ëv, p. 28-29; "Ivanovo Region (Russia)", *FOTW Flags of the World*, http://www.crwflags.com/FOTW/flags/ru-iva.html, accessed 27 June 2008.

Jewish Autonomous Oblast
Еврейская автономная область / Evreiskaia avtonomnaia oblast'

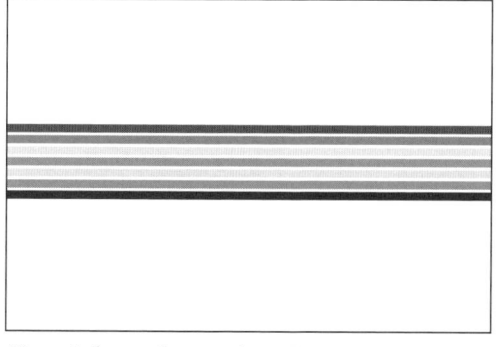

Year Adopted: 1996   **Proportions:** 2:3
Designer: Aleksandr Dmitrievich Valiaev

Federal District: Far Eastern
Administrative Center: Birobidzhan
Population: 185,412

    The field of the Jewish Autonomous Oblast's flag is white. In the center, running horizontally across the length of the flag, are seven narrow lines in rainbow colors—red, orange, yellow, green, light blue, dark blue, and violet. The width of each is 1/40 the width of the flag. They are separated by white fimbriations, 1/120 the width of the flag. White represents purity of thoughts, bright prospects for undertakings and deeds, and the honored fulfillment of duty. The rainbow is a biblical symbol of peace, happiness, and good. In addition, the seven stripes of the rainbow are reminiscent of the seven candles of a menorah, a national and religious symbol of the Jewish people.

Sources: Evreiskaia avtonomnaia oblast', "Simvolika", http://www.eao.ru/?p=5, accessed 15 June 2008; "Flag Evreiskoi avtonomnoi oblasti", *Geral'dika.ru*, http://geraldika.ru/symbols/523, accessed 18 June 2008; "Evreiskaia avtonomnaia oblast'", *Vexillographia: Flagi Rossii*, http://www.vexillographia.ru/russia/subjects/ewish.htm, accessed 1 August 2008; Borisov and Kozina, p. 344; Saprykov (2004), p. 85; Saprykov (2006), p. 85; Smetannikov, p. 96; Solov'ëv, p. 204-205; "Jewish Autonomous Region (Russia)", *FOTW Flags of the World*, http://www.crwflags.com/FOTW/flags/ru-yev.html, accessed 27 June 2008.

Kabardino-Balkaria (Kabardino-Balkar Republic)
Кабардино-Балкарская Республика / Kabardino-Balkarskaia Respublika

Year Adopted: 1994   **Proportions:** 2:3
Designer: unknown

Federal District: Southern
Capital: Nalchik
Population: 892,389

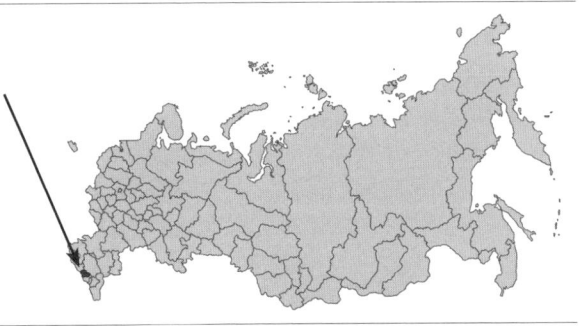

The flag of Kabardino-Balkaria has equal horizontal stripes of light blue, white, and green. Centered in the white stripe is a circular emblem divided horizontally into blue and green halves. In the center of the blue section is a stylized representation of Mount Elbrus in white. Mount Elbrus, located in the republic, is the highest mountain in the Caucasus range and in Europe. Light blue symbolizes the glory of the ancestors of the Kabardins and the Balkars, the honor of the inhabitants, loyalty, and sincerity. White stands for peaceful nature and goodness. Green represents freedom in ideas and affairs, acts, pleasure of dialogue and understanding, and hope for a bright future.

Sources: Kabardino-Balkarskaia Respublika, "Simvolika Kabardino-Balkarskoi Respubliki", http://www.presidentkbr.ru/kbr/symbolism/, accessed 23 June 2008; "Flag Kabardino-Balkarskoi Respubliki", *Geral'dika.ru*, http://geraldika.ru/symbols/210, accessed 17 June 2008; "Kabardino-Balkariia", *Vexillographia: Flagi Rossii*, http://www.vexillographia.ru/russia/subjects/kabarda.htm, accessed 1 August 2008; Borisov and Kozina, p. 34; Saprykov (2004), p. 17; Saprykov (2006), p. 14; Sharkov, p. 38-41, 131-134; Smetannikov, p. 24; Solov'ëv, p. 88-89; "Kabard-Balkaria (Russia)", *FOTW Flags of the World*, http://www.crwflags.com/FOTW/flags/ru-kb.html, accessed 27 June 2008.

Kaliningrad Oblast
Калининградская область / Kaliningradskaia oblast'

Year Adopted: 2006 **Proportions:** 2:3
Designer: unknown

Federal District: Northwestern
Administrative Center:
 Kaliningrad
Population: 937,360

The flag of Kaliningrad Oblast has three horizontal stripes: red over yellow over blue, with the central stripe 1/3 the width of the others. In the upper hoist is a white fortress with an open gate. Above the fortress is a yellow monogram of Empress Elizabeth Petrovna (ruled 1741-62). The colors come from the arms of the oblast where red is a symbol of labor, vitality, strength, courage, selflessness, heroism of the Russian soldier, and as a tribute to those who have fallen in defense of the territory. Blue represents beauty, love, peace, and lofty aspirations. Yellow symbolizes greatness, wealth, constancy, durability, and power. The fortress is a symbol of confidence, steadfastness, and defense preparedness; the open gate stands for hospitality, friendly intentions, and contacts with foreign countries near and far. In addition, the monogram emphasizes the historical links of present-day Kaliningrad with Russia during the 18th century.

Sources: Kaliningradskaia oblast', "Ofitsial'naya simvolika", http://gov.kaliningrad.ru/index.php?d2m=page&contid=887309d048beef83ad3eabf2a79a64a389ab1c9f, accessed 14 June 2008; "Flag Kaliningradskoi oblasti", *Geral'dika.ru*, http://geraldika.ru/symbols/1791, accessed 19 June 2008; "Kaliningradskaia oblast'", *Vexillographia: Flagi Rossii*, http://www.vexillographia.ru/russia/subjects/kalinin.htm, accessed 1 August 2008; Borisov and Kozina, p. 142; Smetannikov, p. 56; Solov'ëv, p. 66-67; "Kaliningrad Region (Russia)", *FOTW Flags of the World*, http://www.crwflags.com/FOTW/flags/ru-39.html, accessed 27 June 2008.

Kalmykia, Republic of
Республика Калмыкия / Respublika Kalmykiia

Year Adopted: 1993   **Proportions:** 1:2; changed from 2:7 in 1996
Designer: B. B. Erdniev

Federal District: Southern
Capital: Elista
Population: 284,001

Kalmykia's flag has a yellow field with a light blue disk in the center bearing a stylized lotus flower with nine petals. Yellow represents the people, their religious beliefs, and the sun shining on the republic. The blue disk (approximately 2/3 the height of the flag) with the lotus represents the road to a bright future, prosperity, and the well-being and happiness of the people. In addition, the upper five petals of the lotus symbolize five continents of the globe; the lower four represent the aspiration of the republic's people for friendship and cooperation with all the nations of the world. The lotus is also a traditional symbol of Buddhism, the predominant religion in the region.

For a brief period (1992-93) another flag was used. It consisted of three horizontal stripes—azure blue, yellow, and red in proportions of 1:2:1; in the center of the yellow stripe was a symbol in red from old Mongolian script which meant Kalmuk. The first flag was based upon the tricolor of the Don Cossacks and was designed by P. Bitkeevym.

Sources: Respublika Kalmykiia, "O gosudarstvennykh simvolakh Respubliki Kalmykiia", http://kalm.ru/en/docs_view.php?id=81, accessed 21 May 2008; "Flag Respubliki Kalmykiia", *Geral'dika.ru*, http://geraldika.ru/symbols/223, accessed 17 June 2008; "Kalmykiia", *Vexillographia: Flagi Rossii*, http://www.vexillographia.ru/russia/subjects/kalmyk.htm, accessed 1 August 2008; Borisov and Kozina, p. 35-36; Saprykov (2004), p. 18; Saprykov (2006), p. 15; Sharkov, p. 42-45, 135-138; Smetannikov, p. 25; Solov'ëv, p. 90-91; "Kalmykia (Russia)", *FOTW Flags of the World*, http://www.crwflags.com/FOTW/flags/ru-08.html, accessed 27 June 2008; "Don Cossacks", *Wikipedia*, http://en.wikipedia.org/wiki/Don_Cossacks, accessed 10 August 2008. The image of the flag of Kalmykia (1992-93) was provided by Victor Lomantsov from the *Vexillographia* website, http://vexillographia.ru.

Kaluga Oblast
Калужская область / Kaluzhskaia oblast'

Year Adopted: 2004 **Proportions:** 2:3
Designer: unknown

Federal District: Central
Administrative Center: Kaluga
Population: 1,002,859

Kaluga Oblast has a flag with three horizontal stripes. The top and bottom stripes are of equal width and are red and green. Separating these stripes is a band of silver (often shown as white) 1/6 the width of the flag. Red is a symbol of fearlessness, strength, and the desire to protect the fatherland. Green represents hope, youth, and peace, and in Orthodox tradition is the color of festive clothing. Silver (or white) symbolizes light, purity of thoughts, the Oka River, and the belt of the Virgin Mary, protector of the land of Russia. Centered on the red stripe is an imperial crown in gold, reflecting that in the 19th century the region had the status of a *guberniya* or imperial province.

Sources: Kaluzhskaia oblast', "O flage Kaluzhskoi", http://www.admobl.kaluga.ru/New/Law/flag.htm, accessed 26 June 2008; "Flag Kaluzhskoi oblasti", *Geral'dika.ru*, http://geraldika.ru/symbols/1590, accessed 19 June 2008; "Kaluzhskaia oblast'", *Vexillographia: Flagi Rossii*, http://www.vexillographia.ru/russia/subjects/kaluga.htm, accessed 1 August 2008; Saprykov (2004), p. 47; Saprykov (2006), p. 46; Smetannikov, p. 57; Solov'ëv, p. 30-31; "Kaluga Region (Russia)", *FOTW Flags of the World*, http://www.crwflags.com/FOTW/flags/ru-40.html, accessed 27 June 2008.

Kamchatka Krai
Камчатский край / Kamchatskii krai

No flag

Federal District: Far Eastern
Administrative Center:
  Petropavlovsk-Kamchatsky
Population: 343,539

Kamchatka Krai was formed by the merger of Kamchatka Oblast and Koryak Autonomous Okrug on 1 July 2007. A commission has been formed to create new symbols. The commission has held a design contest, but a new flag had not yet been adopted at press time. In the absence of a new flag for Kamchatka Krai, the old flags of Kamchatka Oblast and Koryak Autonomous Okrug continue to be used in those regions. See the "Flags of Merged Federal Subjects" section for information on these flags.

Sources: "U Kamchatskogo kraia poiaviatsia gimn, flag i gerb", *Regnum Informatsionnoe Agentstvo* (23 May 2008), http://www.regnum.ru/news/1004429.html, accessed 24 June 2008; "Za luchshii eskiz gerba i flaga Kamchatskogo kraia dadut 50 tysiach rublei", *Regnum Informatsionnoe Agentstvo* (19 August 2008), http://www.regnum.ru/news/1043272.html, accessed 12 September 2008; "Kamchatskii krai obretet sobstvennyi gimn, flag i gerb", *Sever DB Informatsionnoe Agentstvo* (23 May 2008), http://severdv.ru/news/show/?id=8979, accessed 12 September 2008; "Gimn, gerb i flag dlia Kamchatki", *DV Reclama* (18 August 2008), http://www.dv-reclama.ru/?id=4207, accessed 12 September 2008.

Karachay-Cherkessia (Karachay-Cherkess Republic)
Карачаево-Черкесская Республика / Karachaevo-Cherkesskaia Respublika

Year Adopted: 1994   **Proportions:** 2:3; changed from 1:2 in 1996
Designer: Nazir K. Kushkhov

Federal District: Southern
Capital: Cherkessk
Population: 427,194

The flag of Karachay-Cherkessia consists of three equal horizontal stripes of blue, green, and red. In the center of the green stripe is a yellow circle encompassing a scene of a sunrise behind Mount Elbrus, the highest peak in the Caucasus Mountains and in Europe. Blue symbolizes bright and good motives, peace, and calmness. Green symbolizes nature, fertility, riches, creation, and is the color of youth, wisdom, and restraint. Red is a solemn color and represents warmth and closeness between people.

Sources: Karachaevo-Cherkesskaia Respublika, "Simvoly KChR," http://www.kchr.info/simbols.html, accessed 13 June 2008; "Flag Karachaevo-Cherkesskoi Respubliki", *Geral'dika.ru*, http://geraldika.ru/symbols/231, accessed 17 June 2008; "Karachaevo-Cherkesiia", *Vexillographia: Flagi Rossii*, http://www.vexillographia.ru/russia/subjects/karacaj.htm, accessed 1 August 2008; Borisov and Kozina, p. 37; Saprykov (2004), p. 19; Saprykov (2006), p. 16; Sharkov, p. 46-48, 139-141, [196-200], [203-207]; Smetannikov, p. 26; Solov'ëv, p. 92-93; "Karachay-Cherkessia (Russia)", *FOTW Flags of the World*, http://www.crwflags.com/FOTW/flags/ru-kc.html, accessed 27 June 2008.

Karelia, Republic of
Республика Карелия / Respublika Kareliia

Year Adopted: 1993   **Proportions:** 2:3; changed from 1:2 in 1997
Designer: A. I. Kinner

Federal District: Northwestern
Capital: Petrozavodsk
Population: 687,500

Karelia's flag has equal horizontal stripes of red, light blue, and green. Red stands for the strength and courage of the people, and is also reminiscent of traditional red-on-white Karelian embroidery. Green and blue represent the environment of Karelia—woods, lakes, and rivers. Blue not only symbolizes water, but also represents greatness and beauty. Green also personifies hope and a belief in happiness. The order of the stripes is based on the historic flag of the Karelo-Finnish Soviet Socialist Republic from the 1940s and 1950s—a Soviet-style flag with a red field, yellow hammer and sickle at the hoist, and light blue and green stripes at the bottom.

Sources: Respublika Kareliia, "Gosudarstvennyi Flag Respubliki Kareliia", http://gov.karelia.ru/gov/flag.html, accessed 13 June; Respublika Kareliia, "Istoricheskaia spravka ob ofitsial'nykh simvolakh Respubliki Kareliia, http://gov.karelia.ru/gov/Different/Symbolics/flag_hist.html, accessed 1 July 2008; "Flag Respubliki Kareliia", *Geral'dika.ru*, http://geraldika.ru/symbols/233, accessed 17 June 2008; "Kareliia", *Vexillographia: Flagi Rossii*, http://www.vexillographia.ru/russia/subjects/karelia.html, accessed 1 August 2008; Borisov and Kozina, p. 38; Saprykov (2004), p. 20; Saprykov (2006), p. 17; Sharkov, p. 49-52, 142-145; Smetannikov, p. 27; Solov'ëv, p. 58-59; "Karelia (Russia)", *FOTW Flags of the World*, http://www.crwflags.com/FOTW/flags/ru-10.html, accessed 27 June 2008.

Kemerovo Oblast
Кемеровская область / Kemerovskaia oblast'

Year Adopted: 2002 **Proportions:** 2:3
Designer: unknown

Federal District: Siberian
Administrative Center: Kemerovo
Largest City: Novokuznetsk
Population: 2,821,859

The flag of Kemerovo Oblast has two vertical stripes—blue at the hoist (1/3 the length) and red at the fly (2/3 the length). The colors of the flag are taken from the old flag of the Russian SFSR. In the upper hoist are the arms of the oblast. Symbols on the arms include a hammer and pick (symbols of industry) and three stalks of wheat (symbols of agriculture). The arms are topped with a crown in the form of a stylized full bowl, which represents the mines of the Kuznetsk Basin (often abbreviated as Kuzbass).

Sources: Kemerovskaia oblast', "Simvolika Kemerovskoi oblasti", http://www.ako.ru/Official/simbols.asp?n=8, accessed 14 June 2008; "Flag Kemerovskoi oblasti", *Geral'dika.ru*, http://geraldika.ru/symbols/1588, accessed 19 June 2008; "Kemerovskaia oblast'", *Vexillographia: Flagi Rossii*, http://www.vexillographia.ru/russia/subjects/kemerovo.htm, accessed 1 August 2008; Borisov and Kozina, p. 152; Saprykov (2004), p. 49; Saprykov (2006), p. 48; Smetannikov, p. 59; Solov'ëv, p. 170-171 "Kemerovo Region (Russia)", *FOTW Flags of the World*, http://www.crwflags.com/FOTW/flags/ru-42.html, accessed 27 June 2008.

Khabarovsk Krai
Хабаровский край / Khabarovskii krai

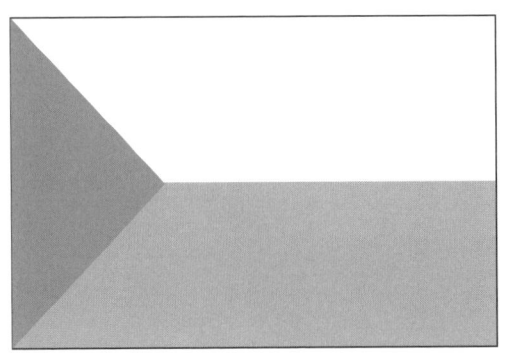

Year Adopted: 1994   **Proportions:** 2:3
Designer: Sergei N. Loginov

Federal District: Far Eastern
Administrative Center:
  Khabarovsk
Population: 1,401,915

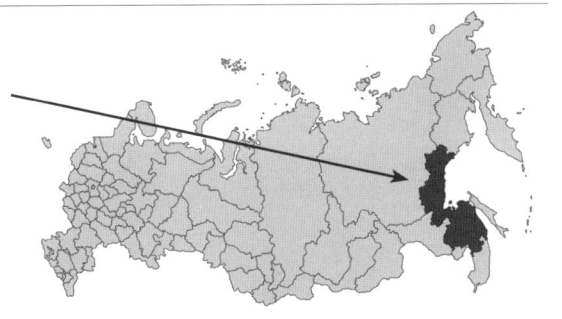

The flag of Khabarovsk Krai is divided into three sections. At the hoist is a green isosceles triangle; at the fly are two horizontal stripes—white over blue. Green symbolizes hope, joy, and abundance, and also is reminiscent of the flora of the territory and the "endless sea of the taiga". White is a symbol of purity, goodness, and innocence. On the flag, it represents the cloudless peaceful sky, and the pure thoughts of the inhabitants. Blue symbolizes beauty, gentleness, greatness, and the extensive water resources of the territory.

Sources: Khabarovskii krai, "Simvolika Khabarovskogo kraia", http://www.khabkrai.ru/about/symbolism.html, accessed 14 June 2008; "Flag Khabarovskogo kraia", *Geral'dika.ru*, http://geraldika.ru/symbols/470, accessed 18 June 2008; "Khabarovskii krai", *Vexillographia: Flagi Rossii*, http://www.vexillographia.ru/russia/subjects/khabara.htm, accessed 1 August 2008; Borisov and Kozina, p. 89; Saprykov (2004), p. 36; Saprykov (2006), p. 34; Smetannikov, p. 44; Solov'ev, p. 194-195; "Khabarovsk Territory (Russia)", *FOTW Flags of the World*, http://www.crwflags.com/FOTW/flags/ru-kha.html, accessed 27 June 2008.

Khakassia, Republic of
Республика Хакасия / Respublika Khakasiia

Year Adopted: 2002   **Proportions:** 1:2
Designers: Sergei Andreevich Donskov and Gennadii Afrikanovich Viatkin

Federal District: Siberian
Capital: Abakan
Population: 538,054

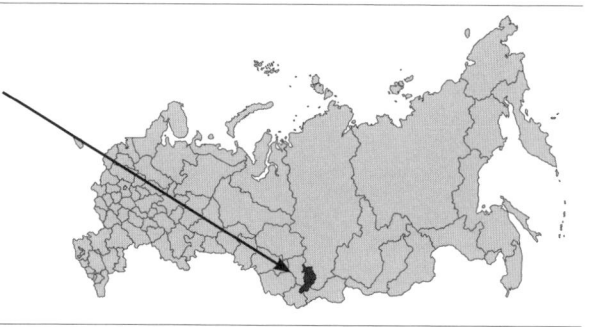

The flag of Khakassia has a green stripe at the hoist and three equal horizontal stripes (blue over white over red) which comprise the remainder of the field. Centered in the green stripe is a golden solar sign, a traditional symbol found on stone sculptures in the republic. This symbol represents the universe and honors the generations of Khakas people who have lived in the region. Green is a traditional color of Siberia and its placement uniting the three stripes symbolizes the connection of modern Khakas to their distant ancestors. It also represents eternal life; the color of the taiga, steppe, and meadows; revival; and the friendship and brotherhood of the people. The colors of the horizontal stripes are from the national flag and emphasize the role of Khakassia as a federal subject of the Russian Federation.

When the flag was first adopted in 1992, the solar sign was black and the stripes were ordered white, blue, and red. The color of the solar sign was changed in 1993, and the stripes were changed to the current order in 2002. This final change was made because of a federal law barring federal subjects from incorporating the national flag into their own flags.

Sources: Respublika Khakasiia, "Gosudarstvennye simvoly Respubliki Khakasiia i Rossiiskoi Federatsii", http://www.rhlider.ru/about-republic/armory/, accessed 14 June 2008; "Flag Respubliki Khakasiia", *Geral'dika.ru*, http://geraldika.ru/symbols/401, accessed 17 June 2008; "Flag Respubliki Khakasiia (1992 g.)", *Geraldika.ru*, http://geraldika.ru/symbols/4603, accessed 10 August 2008; "Khakasiia", *Vexillographia: Flagi Rossii*, http://www.vexillographia.ru/russia/subjects/khakass.htm, accessed 1 August 2008; Borisov and Kozina, p. 60; Saprykov (2004), p. 29; Saprykov (2006), p. 26; Sharkov, p. 88, 181; Smetannikov, p. 36; Solov'ëv, p. 162-163; "Khakassia (Russia)', *FOTW Flags of the World*, http://www.crwflags.com/FOTW/flags/ru-19.html, accessed 27 June 2008.

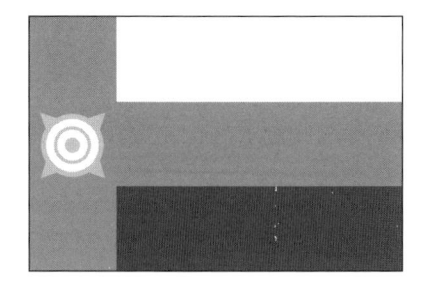

Khanty-Mansi Autonomous Okrug
Ханты-Мансийский автономный округ / Khanty-Mansiiskii avtonomnyi okrug

Year Adopted: 1995 **Proportions:** 1:2
Designer: unknown

Federal District: Urals
Administrative Center: Khanty-Mansiysk
Largest City: Surgut
Population: 1,519,962

Khanty-Mansi Autonomous Okrug (or Khantia-Mansia) has a flag with two horizontal stripes of blue over green and a narrow white vertical stripe at the fly, 1/20 of its length. The colors of the flag represent the geographical features of the region—blue for the water in the rivers and lakes, green for the forests, and white for the snow that covers the region over 200 days a year. In the upper hoist is a symbol from the arms—the main element of the national ornament. This emblem is reminiscent of the antlers of a reindeer, an animal central to the culture of the people.

Sources: Khanty-Mansiiskii avtonomnii okruga, "Zakon Khanty-Mansiiskogo avtonomnogo okruga - Iugry 'O gerbe i flage Khanty-Mansiiskogo avtonomnogo okruga - Iugry'", http://www.dumahmao.ru/generalinformation/lawhmao/, accessed 15 June 2008; "Flag Khanty-Mansiiskogo avtonomnogo okruga", *Geral'dika.ru*, http://geraldika.ru/symbols/536, accessed 18 June 2008; "Khanty-Mansiiskii avtonomnyi okrug - Iugra", *Vexillographia: Flagi Rossii*, http://www.vexillographia.ru/russia/subjects/khanty.htm, accessed 1 August 2008; Borisov and Kozina, p. 400; Saprykov (2004), p. 92; Saprykov (2006), p. 92; Smetannikov, p. 103; Solov'ëv, p. 150-151; "Yugra (Russia)", *FOTW Flags of the World*, http://www.crwflags.com/FOTW/flags/ru-86.html, accessed 27 June 2008.

Kirov Oblast
Кировская область / Kirovskaia oblast'

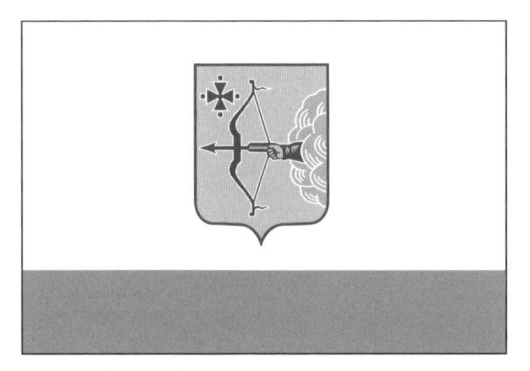

Year Adopted: 2003   **Proportions:** 2:3
Designers: Sergei Iur'evich Gorbachev and Aleksandr Ivanovich Veprikov

Federal District: Volga
Administrative Center: Kirov
Population: 1,401,201

    Kirov Oblast's flag is white with two stripes, green and blue, at its base, each 1/8 the flag's width. White represents the purity of moral foundations, goodness, and modesty, as well as the snow of winter. Green is a symbol of hope, joy, and health. In addition, green stands for the fertility of the land and riches of the forest. Blue symbolizes faithfulness, honesty, and faultlessness; and also represents the Vyatka River. Centered in the white field are the arms of the oblast, placed so that the edges are 1/8 the width of the flag from the top and bottom of the field. On the arms a right hand extends from the clouds holding a drawn bow and arrow. In the upper left of the shield is a military cross with arms of equal size. These symbols represent defense of the homeland, and the essential qualities of bravery, courage, and military skill.

Sources: Kirovskaia oblast', "Flag Kirovskoi oblasti", http://www.ako.kirov.ru/region/symbol/symbol_flag.php, accessed 14 June 2008 "Flag Kirovskoi oblasti", *Geral'dika.ru*, http://geraldika.ru/symbols/2989, accessed 19 June 2008; "Kirovskaia oblast'", *Vexillographia: Flagi Rossii*, http://www.vexillographia.ru/russia/subjects/kirov.htm, accessed 1 August 2008; Borisov and Kozina, p. 157; Saprykov (2004), p. 50; Saprykov (2006), p. 49; Smetannikov, p. 60; Solov'ëv, p. 126-127.

Komi Republic
Республика Коми / Respublika Komi

Year Adopted: 1991   **Proportions:** 2:3; changed from 1:2 in 1997
Designer: V. Ia. Serditov

Federal District: Northwestern
Capital: Syktyvkar
Population: 958,544

Komi's flag consists of three equal horizontal stripes of blue over green over white. The colors represent specific geographic features of the republic—the large endless open spaces of the north (blue), the fields of the taiga (green), and the cleanliness of the snow (white). Green also symbolizes hope and abundance, and the rich environment that supports the Komi people. In addition to representing snow, white stands for the northern position of the republic, the equality of the people, and the unity of their cultures.

Sources: Respublika Komi, "Gosudarstvennaia simvolika Respubliki Komi", http://www.rkomi.ru/gosud/simvol/index.phtml, accessed 13 June 2008; "Flag Respubliki Komi", *Geral'dika.ru*, http://geraldika.ru/symbols/260, accessed 17 June 2008; "Komi", *Vexillographia: Flagi Rossii*, http://www.vexillographia.ru/russia/subjects/komi.htm, accessed 1 August 2008; Borisov and Kozina, p. 41; Saprykov (2004), p. 21; Saprykov (2006), p. 18; Sharkov, p. 53-59, 146-152; Smetannikov, p. 28; Solov'ëv, p. 60-61; "Komia (Russia)", *FOTW Flags of the World*, http://www.crwflags.com/FOTW/flags/ru-11.html, accessed 27 June 2008.

Kostroma Oblast
Костромская область / Kostromskaia oblast'

Year Adopted: 2006   **Proportions:** 2:3
Designers: Konstantin Mochenov, Vladimir Neimark, Yuri Smirnov, Iraida Khlebnikova, Yuri Tsirkunov, Mikhail Medvedev, Gleb Kalashnikov, Galina Tunik, Kirill Perekhodenko, Robert Malanichev, Galina Rusanova

Federal District: Central
Administrative Center: Kostroma
Population: 692,315

The flag of Kostroma Oblast has three vertical stripes of red/blue/red in proportions of 1:2:1. Centered in the blue stripe is a galleon from the arms, which Catherine II granted the region in memory of her travels along the Volga. It has an eagle's head at the bow and flies a Russian flag from the era of Alexander II.

An earlier design, used 2000-06, was red with a blue stripe at the hoist, similar to the old flag of the Russian SFSR. The shield from the arms was centered on the red portion, and included the ship on the current flag.

Sources: "Flag Kostromskoi oblasti", *Geral'dika.ru*, http://geraldika.ru/symbols/16177, accessed 19 June 2008; "Flag Kostromskoi oblasti (2000 g.)", *Geral'dika.ru*, http://geraldika.ru/symbols/829, accessed 10 August 2008; "Kostromskaia oblast'", *Vexillographia: Flagi Rossii*, http://www.vexillographia.ru/russia/subjects/kostroma.htm, accessed 1 August 2008; Borisov and Kozina, p. 161; Saprykov (2004), p. 51; Saprykov (2006), p. 50; Smetannikov, p. 61; Solov'ëv, p. 32-33; "Kostroma Region (Russia)", *FOTW Flags of the World*, http://www.crwflags.com/FOTW/flags/ru-44.html, accessed 27 June 2008.

Krasnodar Krai
Краснодарский край / Krasnodarskii krai

Year Adopted: 1995   **Proportions:** 2:3
Designer: N. P. Ishchenko

Federal District: Southern
Administrative Center: Krasnodar
Population: 5,141,852

The flag of Krasnodar Krai has three horizontal stripes—blue over crimson over green in proportions of 1:2:1. Blue represents the Don Cossacks. Crimson stands for the Zaporozhian Cossacks (also known as the Black Sea Cossack Host), credited with founding Kuban, another name for the region. Green symbolizes the fertility and riches of the territory. Centered in the field of the flag is a one-color variant of the territory's arms in yellow with orange outlines. The major elements are the top portion of a two-headed eagle and a fortress. Also in the charge are five monogrammed standards of rulers of the Russian Empire—Alexander I, Catherine II, Alexander II, Paul I, and Nicholas I.

The basic design was adopted in 1995 but altered in 2004 to use a lighter shade of blue. During this time the arms on the flag were also changed so that the background colors of the stripes would show through.

Sources: Krasnodarskii krai, "Flag Krasnodarskogo kraia", http://admkrai.kuban.ru/geraldika/flag.html, accessed 14 June 2008; Krasnodarskii krai, "Gerb Krasnodarskogo kraia', http://admkrai.kuban.ru/geraldika/emblem.html, accessed 13 July 2008; "Flag Krasnodarskogo kraia", *Geral'dika.ru*, http://geraldika.ru/symbols/442, accessed 18 June 2008; "Krasnodarskii krai", *Vexillographia: Flagi Rossii*, http://www.vexillographia.ru/russia/subjects/krasndar.htm, accessed 1 August 2008; Borisov and Kozina, p. 72; Saprykov (2004), p. 32; Saprykov (2006), p. 30; Smetannikov, p. 40; Solov'ëv, p. 98-99 "Krasnodar Territory (Russia)", *FOTW Flags of the World*, http://www.crwflags.com/FOTW/flags/ru-kda.html, accessed 27 June 2008; "Zaporozhian Cossacks", *Wikipedia*, http://en.wikipedia.org/wiki/Zaporozhian_Cossacks, accessed 25 August 2008; "Kuban", *Wikipedia*, http://en.wikipedia.org/wiki/Kuban, accessed 25 August 2008.

Krasnoyarsk Krai
Красноярский край / Krasnoiarskii krai

Year Adopted: 2000 **Proportions:** 2:3
Designer: V. A. Grigor'ev

Federal District: Siberian
Administrative Center: Krasnoyarsk
Population: 2,889,785

Krasnoyarsk Krai's flag is red with the arms of the territory in the center. The height of the arms is 2/3 the height of the hoist. On the arms the principal element is a gold lion holding a shovel in his right paw and a sickle in his left. Behind the lion is a vertical blue stripe set to the left. On top of the shield are three military ribbons. The red color of the field represents courage, bravery, and fearlessness.

Sources: "Krasnoiarskii krai, "Zakon Krasnoiarskogo kraya o flage Krasnoiarskogo kraia", http://www.krskstate.ru/page.aspx?pageid=14239&article=14237, accessed 23 June 2008; "Flag Krasnoiarskogo kraia", *Geral'dika.ru*, http://geraldika.ru/symbols/449, accessed 18 June 2008; "Krasnoiarskii krai", *Vexillographia: Flagi Rossii*, http://www.vexillographia.ru/russia/subjects/krasnjar.htm, accessed 1 August 2008; Borisov and Kozina, p. 78; Saprykov (2004), p. 33; Saprykov (2006), p. 31; Smetannikov, p. 41; Solov'ëv, p. 166-167; "Krasnoyarsk Territory (Russia)", *FOTW Flags of the World*, http://www.crwflags.com/FOTW/flags/ru-24.html, accessed 27 June 2008.

Kurgan Oblast
Курганская область / Kurganskaia oblast'

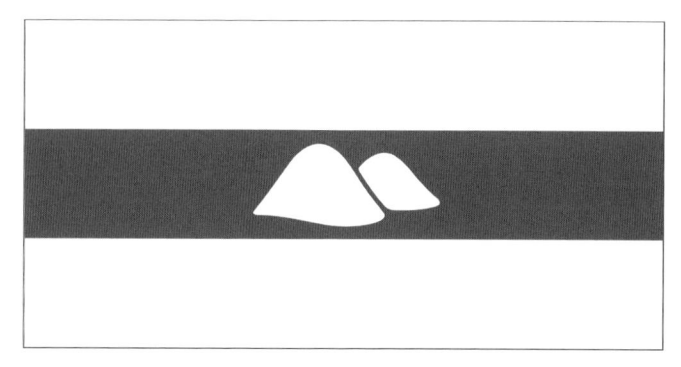

Year Adopted: 1997   **Proportions:** 1:2
Designer: Dmitrii V. Ivanov

Federal District: Urals
Administrative Center: Kurgan
Population: 952,673

Kurgan Oblast has a flag with three equal horizontal stripes—white, emerald green, and white. Green and white have long been the traditional colors of Siberia, a region which is sometimes defined as including Kurgan Oblast. Centered in the green stripe are two white burial mounds. In Russian, the word for this type of barrow is *kurgan*, the source of the oblast's name.

Sources: Kurganskaia oblast', "Geral'dika", http://www.kurganobl.ru/gerald.html, accessed 14 June 2008; "Flag Kurganskoi oblasti", *Geral'dika.ru*, http://geraldika.ru/symbols/835, accessed 20 June 2008; "Kurganskaia oblast'", *Vexillographia: Flagi Rossii*, http://www.vexillographia.ru/russia/subjects/kurgan.htm, accessed 1 August 2008; Borisov and Kozina, p. 164; Saprykov (2004), p. 52; Saprykov (2006), p. 51; Smetannikov, p. 62; Solov'ëv, p. 142-143; "Kurgan Region (Russia)", *FOTW Flags of the World*, http://www.crwflags.com/FOTW/flags/ru-kgn.html, accessed 27 June 2008.

Kursk Oblast
Курская область / Kurskaia oblast'

Year Adopted: 1996   **Proportions:** 2:3
Designer: A. V. Rutskoi

Federal District: Central
Administrative Center: Kursk
Population: 1,155,417

The flag of Kursk Oblast has five horizontal stripes: red, silver, gold, black, and red, in approximate proportions of 1:2:2:2:1. Red represents continuity, as it has appeared on the flags of the Russian Empire, the Soviet Union, and modern Russia. It is also included on the flag as a tribute to the veterans of the Great Patriotic War (World War II). Silver/white represents the purity of the thoughts of the population. Gold/yellow recalls the abundant fields of grain in the region, and black symbolizes *chernozëm*—the fertile black topsoil of central European Russia. On the field of the flag are the arms of the oblast, which feature three silver partridges on a blue diagonal stripe and a field of white. It has been suggested that the name "Kursk" is derived from the word for "partridge"—*kuropatka*, although this explanation is not widely accepted. The shield is topped with a crown.

Sources: Kurskaia oblast', "Zakon Kurskoi oblasti o gerbe i flage Kurskoi oblasti", http://www.rkursk.ru/index1.php?c_tb=1&m_m=3&d_m=2&f_src=zakonodatelstvo/flgbzakon.html, accessed 15 June 2008; "Flag Kurskoi oblasti", *Geral'dika.ru*, http://geraldika.ru/symbols/847, accessed 20 June 2008; "Kurskaia oblast'", *Vexillographia: Flagi Rossii*, http://www.vexillographia.ru/russia/subjects/kursk.htm, accessed 1 August 2008; Borisov and Kozina, p. 167; Saprykov (2004), p. 53; Saprykov (2006), p. 52; Smetannikov, p. 63; Solov'ëv, p. 34-35; "Kursk Region (Russia)", *FOTW Flags of the World*, http://www.crwflags.com/FOTW/flags/ru-46.html, accessed 27 June 2008.

Leningrad Oblast
Ленинградская область / Leningradskaia oblast'

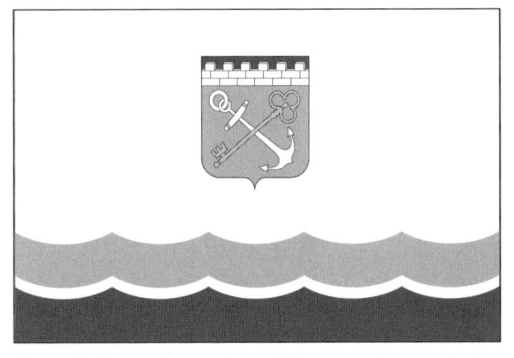

Year Adopted: 1997 **Proportions:** 2:3
Designer: V. I. Evlanov

Federal District: Northwestern
Largest City: Gatchina
Population: 1,631,894

Leningrad Oblast's flag has stripes in the same sequence as the national flag's and represent the oblast's role as a federal subject of the Russian Federation. The upper two-thirds of the flag are white with waves of blue and red (each 1/6 of the flag's width at the hoist) running along the bottom. These blue and red waves are separated by a white fimbriation. Centered in the white area are the arms of the oblast, which show a silver anchor crossed by a gold key in front of a white fortified wall, on a field of blue. The anchor represents the role of the oblast as a seaport, while the key symbolizes how Russia gained access to the West through the Baltic Sea. In addition, the fortress wall illustrates the role of this region in guaranteeing the security of Russia.

Sources: Leningradskaia oblast', "Zakon o gerbe i flage Leningradskoi oblasti", http://lenobl.ru/guide/symbol, accessed 15 June 2008; "Flag Leningradskoi oblasti", *Geral'dika.ru,* http://geraldika.ru/symbols/851, accessed 20 June 2008; "Leningradskaia oblast'", *Vexillographia: Flagi Rossii,* http://www.vexillographia.ru/russia/subjects/leningr.htm, accessed 1 August 2008; Borisov and Kozina, p. 170; Saprykov (2004), p. 54; Saprykov (2006), p. 53; Smetannikov, p. 64; Solov'ëv, p. 68-69; "Leningrad Region (Russia)", *FOTW Flags of the World,* http://www.crwflags.com/FOTW/flags/ru-47.html, accessed 27 June 2008.

Lipetsk Oblast
Липецкая область / Lipetskaia oblast'

Year Adopted: 2003   **Proportions:** 2:3
Designers: M. Medvedev, K. Mochenov, R. Malanichev, Iu. Korzhik, G.Tunik

Federal District: Central
Administrative Center: Lipetsk
Population: 1,163,348

The flag of Lipetsk Oblast is an armorial banner of the oblast's arms. It has a red field with five overlapping green hills at the bottom (in height approximately 1/3 the width of the flag). Centered on the hills is a yellow linden tree, an ancient symbol of brotherhood and harmony. Red symbolizes the industry of the region, work, vitality, courage, celebration, and beauty. Green stands for nature in the oblast, plenty, prosperity, and stability. Yellow (gold) represents the sun, wealth, grain, and fertility. All elements in the arms represent the people and their contribution to the economic, cultural, and spiritual development of the region and of the country. Four of the hills represent the regions from which the territory of Lipetsk Oblast was drawn—Voronezh, Oryol, Ryazan, and Kursk; the fifth symbolizes Lipetsk Oblast.

Sources: "Flag Lipetskoi oblasti", *Geral'dika.ru*, http://geraldika.ru/symbols/3781, accessed 20 June 2008; "Gerb Lipetskoi oblasti", *Geral'dika.ru*, http://geraldika.ru/symbols/3780, accessed 6 July 2008; "Lipetskaia oblast", *Vexillographia: Flagi Rossii*, http://www.vexillographia.ru/russia/subjects/lipeck.htm, accessed 1 August 2008; Borisov and Kozina, p. 177; Saprykov (2004), p. 55; Saprykov (2006), p. 54; Smetannikov, p. 65; Solov'ëv, p. 36-37; "Lipetsk Region (Russia)", *FOTW Flags of the World*, http://www.crwflags.com/FOTW/flags/ru-48.html, accessed 27 June 2008.

Magadan Oblast
Магаданская область / Magadanskaia oblast'

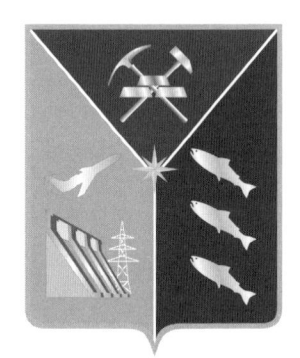

Year Adopted: 2001 **Proportions:** 2:3
Designer: unknown

Federal District: Far Eastern
Administrative Center: Magadan
Population: 162,969

    Magadan Oblast's flag incorporates the national colors of Russia. It has a red field with a series of blue and white waves running horizontally along the bottom 1/4 of the flag. The scalloped points of the lower white waves align with troughs of the upper white waves. These waves represent the oblast's location on Russia's east coast. In the upper hoist are the arms of the oblast. The upper portion of the arms shows a geology hammer and pick behind a pyramid of silver and gold ingots, symbols of prosperity, well-being, and mining—the economic base of the region. In the left portion of the arms are a hydroelectric dam and an airplane. These symbols emphasize the importance of the hydroelectric industry and the connection of Magadan Oblast to the rest of Russia. In the right portion are three golden fish, representing the importance of the fishing industry.

Sources: Magadanskaia oblast', "Simvolika regiona", http://www.magadan.ru/region/gerb.php, accessed 15 June 2008; "Flag Magadanskoi oblasti", *Geral'dika.ru*, http://geraldika.ru/symbols/130, accessed 20 June 2008; "Magadanskaia oblast'", *Vexillographia: Flagi Rossii*, http://www.vexillographia.ru/russia/subjects/magadan.htm, accessed 1 August 2008; Borisov and Kozina, p. 180; Saprykov (2004), p. 56; Saprykov (2006), p. 55; Smetannikov, p. 66; Solov'ëv, p. 200-201; "Magadan Region (Russia)", *FOTW Flags of the World*, http://www.crwflags.com/FOTW/flags/ru-49.html, accessed 27 June 2008.

Mari El Republic
Республика Марий Эл / Respublika Marii-El

Year Adopted: 2006
Proportions: 2:3; changed from 1:2 when redesigned in 2006
Designers: G. N. Bulygin and A. A. Danilov

Federal District: Volga
Capital: Yoshkar-Ola
Population: 700,118

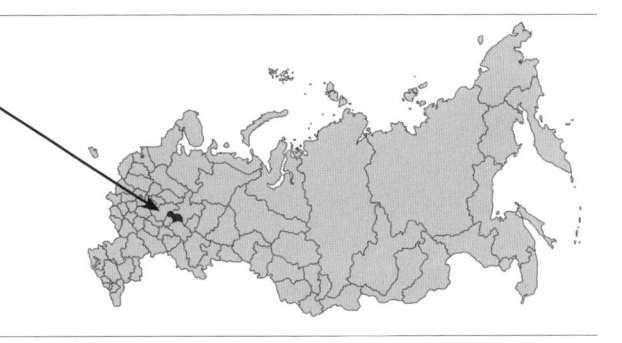

The flag of Mari El consists of three horizontal stripes—blue, white, and red, in proportions of 3:4:3. Centered in the white stripe is a simplified Mari El cross in red (sometimes called a solar symbol in descriptions of the flag). This symbol has long been associated with the agrarian culture of the region and represents the concepts of fertility and eternity. The emblem is 1/3 the width of the flag in size. Blue symbolizes the clean skies over the republic. It also represents water, which was an ancient object of worship for the Mari people. White is the traditional color of labor and a characteristic of the national costume for both everyday use and for celebrations. White also symbolizes life, peace, goodness, fairness, and high morals. Red is widely used in the folk arts of the people and is linked to their spiritual origins.

An earlier version, used from 1992 to

2006, had narrower stripes at the top and bottom. The emblem was of a slightly different design and was closer to the hoist. Under the emblem were the words *Marii El* in Cyrillic letters.

Sources: Respublika Marii El, "Gosudarstvennye simvoly Respubliki Marii El", http://gov.mari.ru/rep/signs.phtml, accessed 13 June 2008; "Flag Respubliki Marii El", *Geral'dika.ru*, http://geraldika.ru/symbols/16978, accessed 17 June 2008; "Flag Respubliki Marii El (1992 g.)", *Geral'dika.ru*, http://geraldika.ru/symbols/272, accessed 10 August 2008; "Marii El", *Vexillographia: Flagi Rossii*, http://www.vexillographia.ru/russia/subjects/marii.htm, accessed 1 August 2008; Borisov and Kozina, p. 43; Saprykov (2004), p. 22; Saprykov (2006), p. 19; Sharkov, p. 60-63, 153-156; Smetannikov, p. 29; Solov'ëv, p. 112-113; "Mariy-El (Russia)", *FOTW Flags of the World*, http://www.crwflags.com/FOTW/flags/ru-12.html, accessed 27 June 2008.

Mordovia, Republic of
Республика Мордовия / Respublika Mordoviia

Year Adopted: 1995 **Proportions:** 2:3; changed from 1:2 in 2008
Designer: Andrei Stepanovich Alëshkin

Federal District: Volga
Capital: Saransk
Population: 833,031

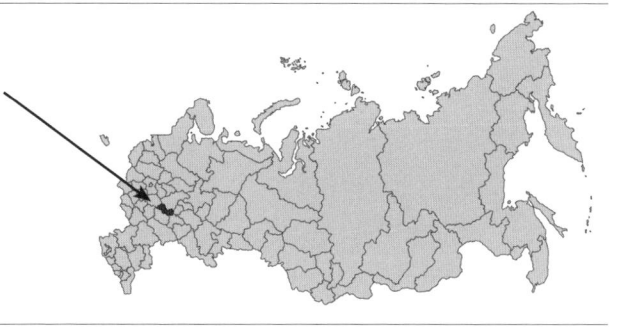

Mordovia, or Mordvinia, has a flag that is a horizontal tricolor of red over white over blue. The top and bottom stripes are each 1/4 the width of the flag. Centered in the white stripe is a solar symbol in red. The emblem consists of four equal segments, resembling arrow fletches, which point toward the center. The colors of the flag derive from the traditional national costume of the republic. Red symbolizes creation and life. White represents spirituality, as well as purity of intentions and thoughts. Blue is a symbol of the fertility of soil when it is damp with moisture. The solar sign not only represents the sun, but also stands for warmth, goodness, and openness. Four portions making up the one symbol emphasizes the unity of the major ethnic groups in the republic—the Moksha and Erzya groups of the Mordvin people, the Russians, and the Tatars—which has led to balance and stability in the region.

Sources: "Flag Respubliki Mordoviia", *Geral'dika.ru*, http://geraldika.ru/symbols/280, accessed 17 June 2008; "Mordoviia", *Vexillographia: Flagi Rossii*, http://www.vexillographia.ru/russia/subjects/mordovia.htm, accessed 1 August 2008; Borisov and Kozina, p. 45; Saprykov (2004), p. 23; Saprykov (2006), p. 20; Sharkov, p. 64-65, 157-158; Smetannikov, p. 30; Solov'ëv, p. 114-115; "Mordovia (Russia)", *FOTW Flags of the World*, http://www.crwflags.com/FOTW/flags/ru-mo.html, accessed 27 June 2008.

Moscow (city)
Москва / Moskva

Year Adopted: 1995 **Proportions:** 2:3
Designer: K. K. Ivanov

Federal District: Central
Population: 10,508,971

The flag of Moscow is drawn from the shield of the traditional arms of the city. It is dark red with an image of St. George the Victorious in the center. Dressed in armor and a blue cape, he rides a white horse and is slaying a dragon. The current arms are based upon a version adopted in 1781. It is believed that the colors of the field, horse, and cape were the basis for the national colors of Russia. St. George, the traditional patron saint of Moscow, was replaced by a socialist design during the Soviet period. The traditional arms were restored after the breakup of the Soviet Union.

Sources: Pravitel'stvo Moskvy, "Ofitsial'nye simvoly", http://www.mos.ru/wps/portal/WebContent?rubricId=2344, accessed 15 June 2008; "Flag goroda Moskva", *Geral'dika.ru*, http://geraldika.ru/symbols/301, accessed 18 June 2008; "Moskva", *Vexillographia: Flagi Rossii*, http://www.vexillographia.ru/russia/subjects/moscow.htm, accessed 1 August 2008; Borisov and Kozina, p. 348; Saprykov (2004), p. 83; Saprykov (2006), p. 83; Smetannikov, p. 94; Solov'ëv, p. 54-55; "Moscow City (Russia)", *FOTW Flags of the World*, http://www.crwflags.com/FOTW/flags/ru-mow.html, accessed 27 June 2008.

Moscow Oblast
Московская область / Moskovskaia oblast'

Year Adopted: 1999   **Proportions:** 2:3
Designer: unknown

Federal District: Central
Largest City: Balashikha
Population: 6,712,582

The flag of Moscow Oblast has a red field with the central emblem from the oblast's arms in the upper hoist. On the emblem is an image of St. George the Victorious, the patron saint of Moscow, riding a white horse and slaying a dragon. The emblem's width is 1/5 the length of the flag. Both the field color and the portrayal of St. George are based upon the historical arms of the city of Moscow.

Sources: Moscovskaia oblast', "Ofitsial'naya simvolika", http://portal.mosreg.ru/formal_symbolism/, accessed 15 June 2008; "Flag Moskovskoi oblasti", *Geral'dika.ru*, http://geraldika.ru/symbols/873, accessed 20 June 2008; "Moskovskaia oblast'", *Vexillographia: Flagi Rossii*, http://www.vexillographia.ru/russia/subjects/mos_obl.htm, accessed 1 August 2008; Borisov and Kozina, p. 182; Saprykov (2004), p. 57; Saprykov (2006), p. 56; Smetannikov, p. 67; Solov'ëv, p. 38-39; "Moscow Region (Russia)", *FOTW Flags of the World*, http://www.crwflags.com/FOTW/flags/ru-mos.html, accessed 27 June 2008.

Murmansk Oblast
Мурманская область / Murmanskaia oblast'

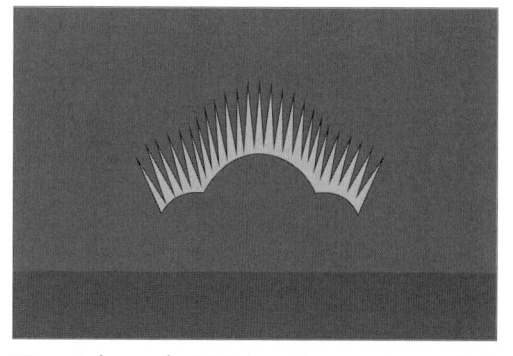

Year Adopted: 2004   **Proportions:** 2:3
Designer: P. Abarin

Federal District: Northwestern
Administrative Center: Murmansk
Population: 842,452

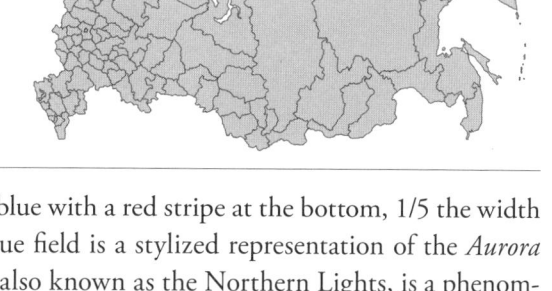

Murmansk Oblast's flag is blue with a red stripe at the bottom, 1/5 the width of the flag. Centered in the blue field is a stylized representation of the *Aurora Borealis* in yellow. The aurora, also known as the Northern Lights, is a phenomenon only visible from the northern latitudes and represents the geographic location of the region. This emblem is 1/2 the length of the flag. Red represents both the concept of life and the progress of the region during the Soviet period. Blue symbolizes beauty, purity, and loyalty. Gold is a symbol of wealth.

Sources: Murmanskaia oblast', "Mnogosvetnyi risunok flaga Murmanskoi oblasti", http://www.gov-murman.ru/symbol/flag/, and "Zakon Murmanskoi oblasti o gerbe i flage Murmanskoi oblasti", http://www.gov-murman.ru/symbol/, accessed 15 June 2008 "Flag Murmanskoi oblasti", *Geral'dika.ru*, http://geraldika.ru/symbols/7312, accessed 20 June 2008; "Murmanskaia oblast'", *Vexillographia: Flagi Rossii*, http://www.vexillographia.ru/russia/subjects/murmansk.htm, accessed 1 August 2008; Saprykov (2006), p. 57; Smetannikov, p. 68; Solov'ëv, p. 70-71; "Murmansk Region (Russia)", *FOTW Flags of the World*, http://www.crwflags.com/FOTW/flags/ru-51.html, accessed 27 June 2008.

Nenets Autonomous Okrug
Ненецкий автономный округ / Nenetskii avtonomnyi okrug

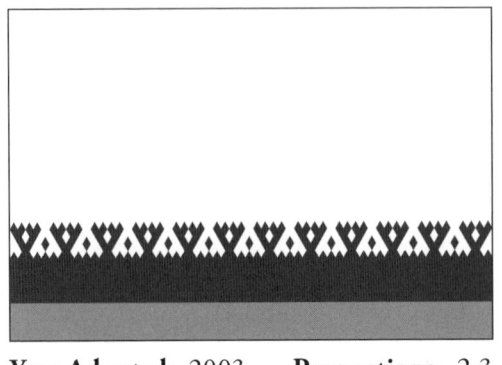

Year Adopted: 2003 **Proportions:** 2:3
Designer: unknown

Federal District: Northwestern
Administrative Center:
  Naryan-Mar
Population: 42,023

The flag of Nenets Autonomous Okrug (or Nenetsia) is white with stripes of blue and green running along its base. The white field occupies about 2/3 the width of the flag, and symbolizes purity, peace of mind, and the primordial nature of the region. Blue represents constancy and infinity. Green symbolizes youth, hope, and vitality. The blue and white stripes are separated by a repeating horizontal design (alternating blue and white) composed of a traditional antler-like ornament from the culture of the region.

Sources: Nenetskii avtonomnii okrug, "Administratsiia Nenetskogo avtonomnogo okruga, http://www.adm-nao.ru/, accessed 26 June 2008 (shows image of flag); "Flag Nenetskogo avtonomnogo okruga", *Geral'dika.ru*, http://geraldika.ru/symbols/1808, accessed 18 June 2008; "Nenetskii avtonomnyi okrug", *Vexillographia: Flagi Rossii*, http://www.vexillographia.ru/russia/subjects/nenets.htm, accessed 1 August 2008; Borisov and Kozina, p. 397; Saprykov (2004), p. 89; Saprykov (2006), p. 89; Smetannikov, p. 100; Solov'ëv, p. 78-79; "Nenetsia (Russia)", *FOTW Flags of the World*, http://www.crwflags.com/FOTW/flags/ru-nen.html, accessed 27 June 2008.

Nizhny Novgorod Oblast
Нижегородская область / Nizhegorodskaia oblast'

Year Adopted: 2005   **Proportions:** 2:3
Designer: unknown

Federal District: Volga
Administrative Center: Nizhny Novgorod
Population: 3,340,684

The flag of Nizhny Novgorod Oblast (or Nizhegorod) is white with the arms of the oblast in the center. White on the flag recalls the banners used by Nizhegorod regiments. The width of the emblem is 2/5 the length of the flag. In the arms the principal element is a scarlet deer; a historical Russian crown tops the arms.

Sources: Nizhegorodskaia oblast', "Flag", http://www.government.nnov.ru/?id=33750, accessed 15 June 2008; "Flag Nizhegorodskoi oblasti", *Geral'dika.ru*, http://geraldika.ru/symbols/11876, accessed 20 June 2008; "Nizhegorodskaia oblast'", *Vexillographia: Flagi Rossii*, http://www.vexillographia.ru/russia/subjects/nizhny.htm, accessed 1 August 2008; Borisov and Kozina, p. 229; Saprykov (2004), p. 58; Saprykov (2006), p. 58; Smetannikov, p. 69; "Nizhniy Novgorod Region (Russia)", *FOTW Flags of the World*, http://www.crwflags.com/FOTW/flags/ru-niz.html, accessed 27 June 2008.

North Ossetia-Alania, Republic of
Республика Северная Осетия-Алания /
Respublika Severnaia Osetiia-Alaniia

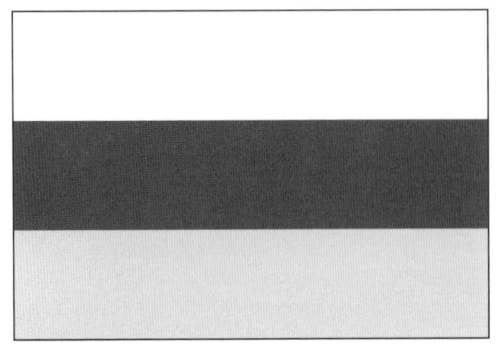

Year Adopted: 1991   **Proportions:** 1:2
Designer: Iu. S. Gagloiti

Federal District: Southern
Capital: Vladikavkaz
Population: 701,807

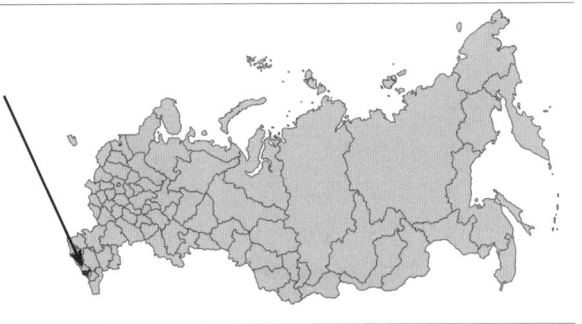

The flag of North Ossetia-Alania has three equal horizontal stripes of white, red, and yellow. White represents moral purity; red stands for military valor; and yellow symbolizes abundance and good fortune. These colors and the concepts they represent are drawn from the historic Scythian and Alan cultures.

Sources: Respublika Severnaia Osetiia-Alaniia, "Ofitsial'naya simvolika", http://www.rso-a.ru/about/detail.php?ID=1387, accessed 14 June 2008; "Flag Respubliki Severnaia Osetiia-Alaniia", *Geral'dika.ru*, http://geraldika.ru/symbols/353, accessed 17 June 2008; "Respublika Severnaia Osetiia - Alaniia", *Vexillographia: Flagi Rossii*, http://www.vexillographia.ru/russia/subjects/sev_oset.htm, accessed 1 August 2008; Borisov and Kozina, p. 50-51; Saprykov (2004), p. 25; Saprykov (2006), p. 22; Sharkov, p. 69-72, 163-166; Smetannikov, p. 32; Solov'ëv, p. 94-95; "North Ossetia (Russia)", *FOTW Flags of the World*, http://www.crwflags.com/FOTW/flags/ru-se.html, accessed 27 June 2008.

Novgorod Oblast
Новгородская область / Novgorodskaia oblast'

Year Adopted: 2007   **Proportions:** 2:3
Designer: unknown

Federal District: Northwestern
Administrative Center: Veliky Novgorod
Population: 645,986

Novgorod Oblast's flag is a vertical tricolor of blue, white, and red in proportions of 1:2:1. Blue stands for devotion, fairness, and constancy, and represents the lakes and rivers of the oblast. White symbolizes aspirations for peace, well-being, and happiness. It is also the color of the cathedrals and monasteries of the region. Red represents the heroic past of the oblast and its antiquity, courage, and beauty. Centered on the white stripe is the shield from the arms of the oblast. In the arms, two black bears support a golden throne. A candlestick tops the throne, and behind the throne are a scepter and cross in gold. At the bottom of the arms are two fish.

Sources: "Flag Novgorodskoi oblasti", *Geral'dika.ru*, http://geraldika.ru/symbols/19893, accessed 20 June 2008; "Novgorodskaia oblast'", *Vexillographia: Flagi Rossii*, http://www.vexillographia.ru/russia/subjects/novgorod.htm, accessed 1 August 2008; Borisov and Kozina, p. 234-235; Saprykov (2004), p. 59; Saprykov (2006), p. 59; Smetannikov, p. 70; "Novgorod Region (Russia)", *FOTW Flags of the World*, http://www.crwflags.com/FOTW/flags/ru-ngr.html, accessed 27 June 2008.

Novosibirsk Oblast
Новосибирская область / Novosibirskaia oblast'

Year Adopted: 2003 **Proportions:** 2:3
Designer: Grigorii Vladimirovich Kuzhelev

Federal District: Siberian
Administrative Center: Novosibirsk
Population: 2,639,857

The flag of Novosibirsk Oblast has vertical stripes: from hoist to fly, red, white, blue, white, and green in approximate proportions of 3:2:1:2:3. Red symbolizes courage, bravery, memories of the heroism of the Novosiberians, and defense of the country. White is for purity, devotion, and faith, and is the color of the Siberian winter. Blue is for the Ob' River, as well as the many lakes and rivers of the region. Green is for hope, abundance, revival, and vitality and also for the natural beauty of the land. Centered on the white and blue stripes are elements from the arms of the oblast, including two black sables, a valuable fur-bearing animal native to the region. They are holding a round loaf of bread, a symbol of hospitality—the peasants of Siberia traditionally offer rye bread and salt to their guests. Below the sables is a narrow line of black/white/black which symbolizes the Trans-Siberian Railway crossing through the territory.

Sources: Novosibirskaia oblast', "Simvolika Novosibirskoi oblasti", http://www3.adm.nso.ru/ru/spr/simvnso/, accessed 15 June 2008; "Flag Novosibirskoi oblasti", *Geral'dika.ru*, http://geraldika.ru/symbols/3415, accessed 20 June 2008; "Novosibirskaia oblast'", *Vexillographia: Flagi Rossii*, http://www.vexillographia.ru/russia/subjects/novosib.htm, accessed 1 August 2008; Borisov and Kozina, p. 237-238; Saprykov (2004), p. 60; Saprykov (2006), p. 60; Smetannikov, p. 71; Solov'ëv, p. 172-173; "Novosibirsk Region (Russia)", *FOTW Flags of the World*, http://www.crwflags.com/FOTW/flags/ru-54.html, accessed 27 June 2008.

Russian Regional Flags C-1

Symbols of the Russian Federation

Russian flag

Russian arms

C-2 *Russian Regional Flags*

Current Symbols of Federal Subjects

Adygea, Republic of

Altai Krai

Altai Republic

Russian Regional Flags C-3

Current Symbols of Federal Subjects

Amur Oblast

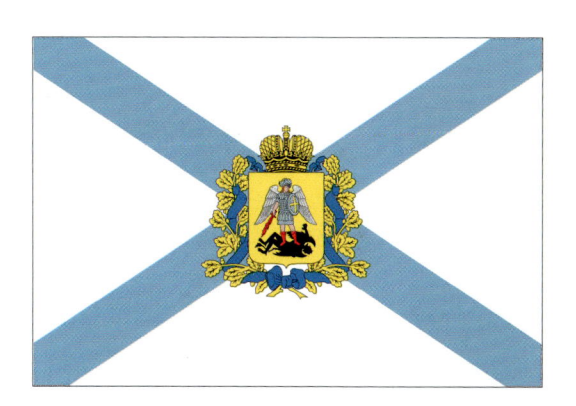

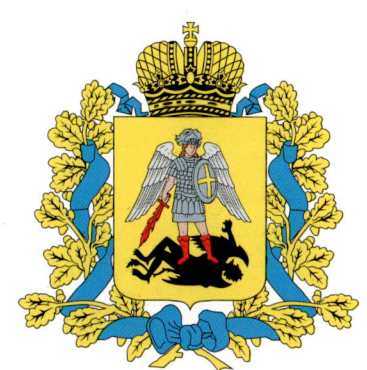

Arkhangelsk Oblast

Astrakhan Oblast

Current Symbols of Federal Subjects

Bashkortostan, Republic of

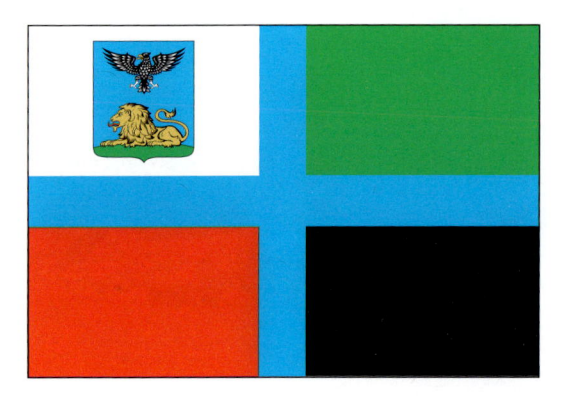

Belgorod Oblast

Bryansk Oblast

Russian Regional Flags   C-5

Current Symbols of Federal Subjects

Buryatia (Buryat Republic)

Chechnya (Chechen Republic)

Chelyabinsk Oblast

C-6 *Russian Regional Flags*

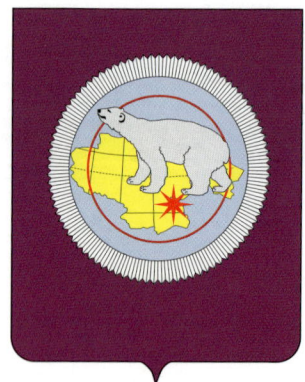

Current Symbols of Federal Subjects

Chukotka Autonomous Okrug

Chuvashia (Chuvash Republic)

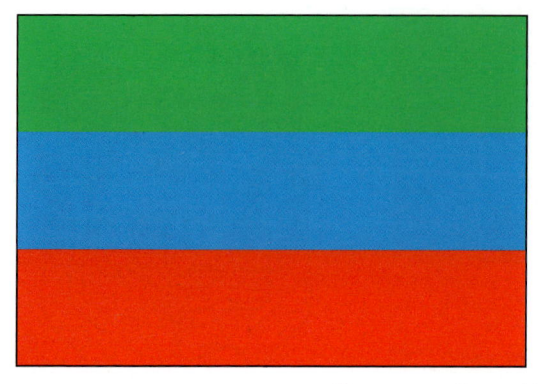

Dagestan, Republic of

Russian Regional Flags   C-7

Current Symbols of Federal Subjects

Ingushetia, Republic of

Irkutsk Oblast

Ivanovo Oblast

C-8   *Russian Regional Flags*

Current Symbols of Federal Subjects

Jewish Autonomous Oblast

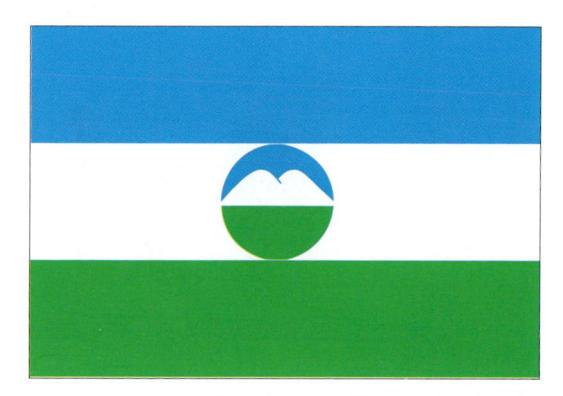

Kabardino-Balkaria (Kabardino-Balkar Republic)

Kaliningrad Oblast

Russian Regional Flags   C-9

Current Symbols of Federal Subjects

Kalmykia, Republic of

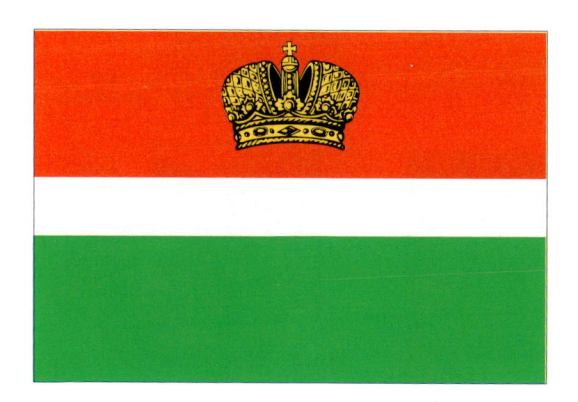

Kaluga Oblast

*Kamchatka Krai has not adopted
a flag or a coat of arms.*

Kamchatka Krai

C-10   Russian Regional Flags

Current Symbols of Federal Subjects

Karachay-Cherkessia (Karachay-Cherkess Republic)

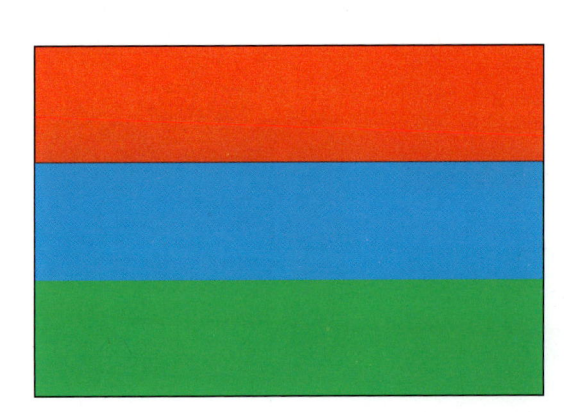

Karelia, Republic of

Kemerovo Oblast

Russian Regional Flags   C-11

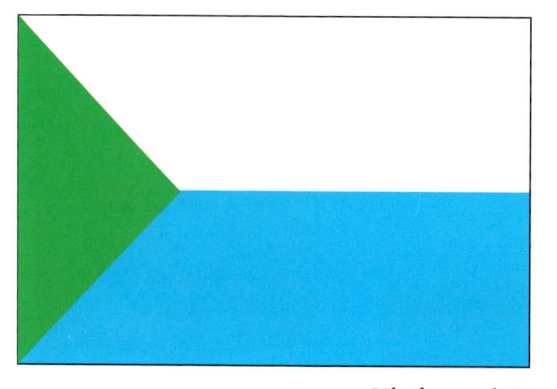

Current Symbols of Federal Subjects

Khabarovsk Krai

Khakassia, Republic of

Khanty-Mansi Autonomous Okrug

C-12 *Russian Regional Flags*

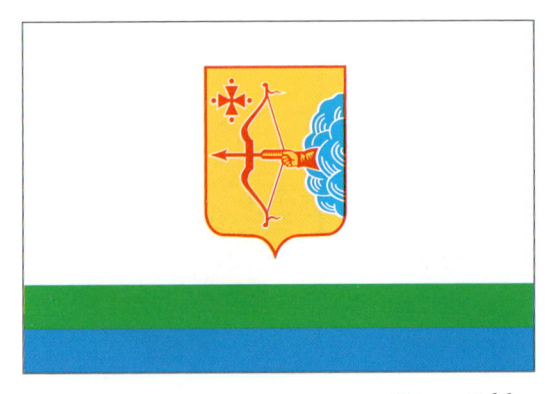

Current Symbols of Federal Subjects

Kirov Oblast

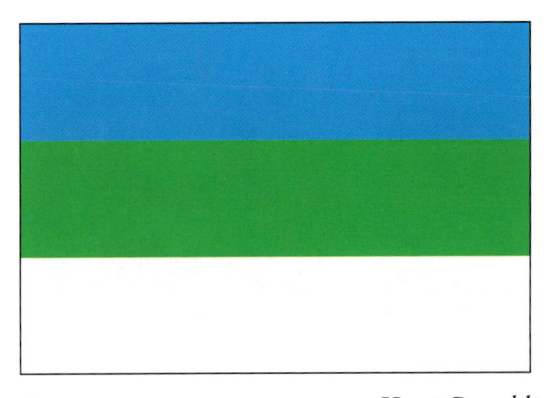

Komi Republic

Kostroma Oblast

Russian Regional Flags   C-13

Current Symbols of Federal Subjects

Krasnodar Krai

Krasnoyarsk Krai

Kurgan Oblast

C-14　*Russian Regional Flags*

Current Symbols of Federal Subjects

Kursk Oblast

Leningrad Oblast

Lipetsk Oblast

Russian Regional Flags   C-15

Current Symbols of Federal Subjects

Magadan Oblast

Mari El Republic

Mordovia, Republic of

C-16 *Russian Regional Flags*

Current Symbols of Federal Subjects

Moscow (city)

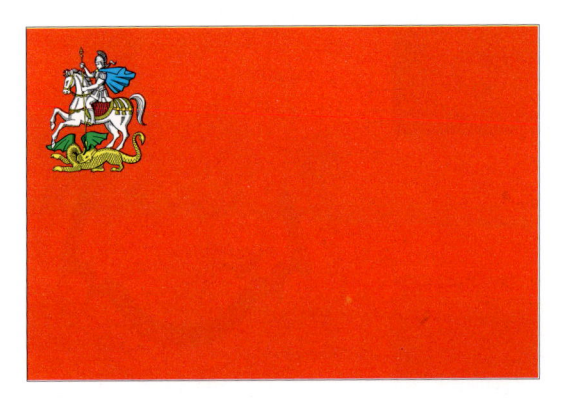

Moscow Oblast

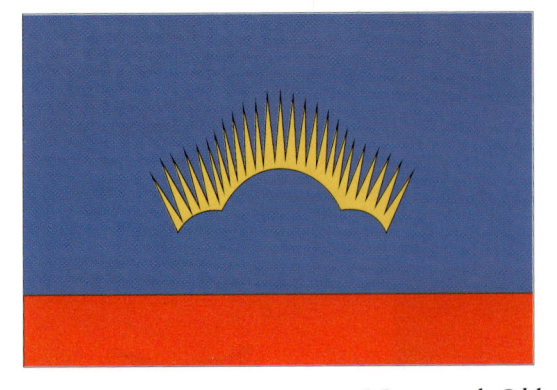

Murmansk Oblast

Russian Regional Flags C-17

Current Symbols of Federal Subjects

Nenets Autonomous Okrug

Nizhny Novgorod Oblast

North Ossetia-Alania, Republic of

C-18 *Russian Regional Flags*

Current Symbols of Federal Subjects

Novgorod Oblast

Novosibirsk Oblast

Omsk Oblast

Russian Regional Flags   C-19

Current Symbols of Federal Subjects

Orenburg Oblast

Oryol Oblast

Penza Oblast

C-20 *Russian Regional Flags*

Current Symbols of Federal Subjects

Perm Krai

Primorsky Krai

Pskov Oblast

Russian Regional Flags   C-21

Current Symbols of Federal Subjects

Rostov Oblast

Ryazan Oblast

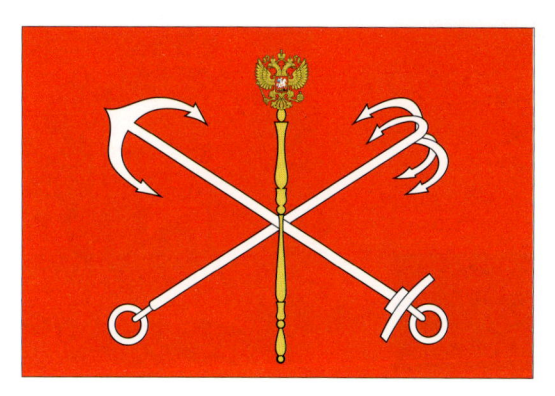

St. Petersburg (city)

Current Symbols of Federal Subjects

Sakha Republic (Yakutia)

Sakhalin Oblast

Samara Oblast

Russian Regional Flags   C-23

Current Symbols of Federal Subjects

Saratov Oblast

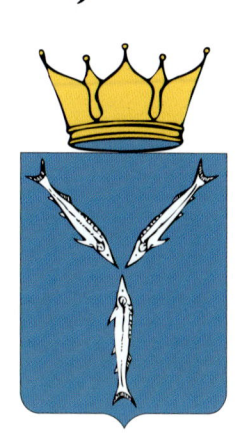

Smolensk Oblast

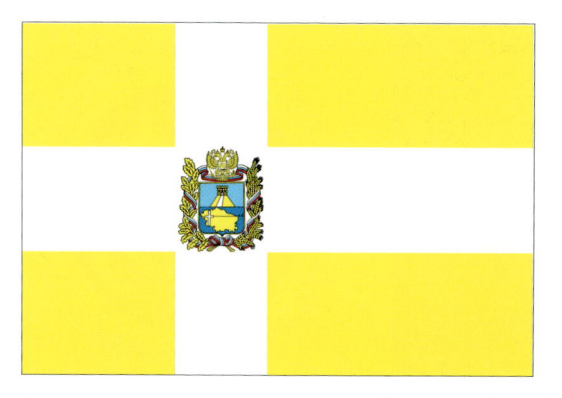

Stavropol Krai

Current Symbols of Federal Subjects

Sverdlovsk Oblast

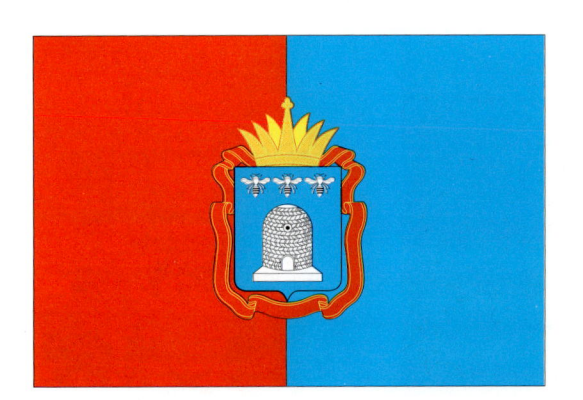

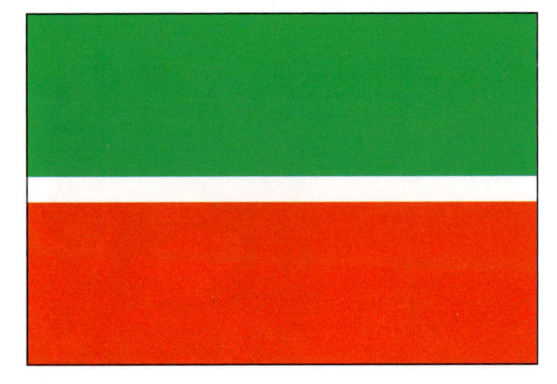

Tambov Oblast

Tatarstan, Republic of

Russian Regional Flags   C-25

Current Symbols of Federal Subjects

Tomsk Oblast

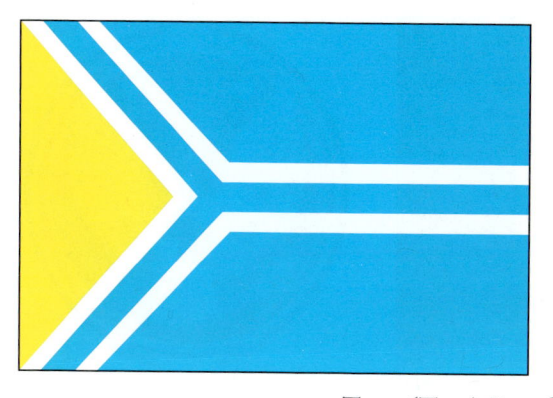

Tula Oblast

Tuva (Tyva) Republic

C-26 *Russian Regional Flags*

Current Symbols of Federal Subjects

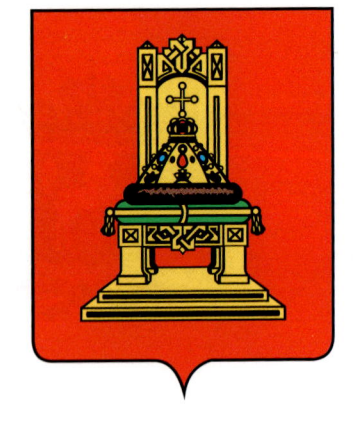

Tver Oblast

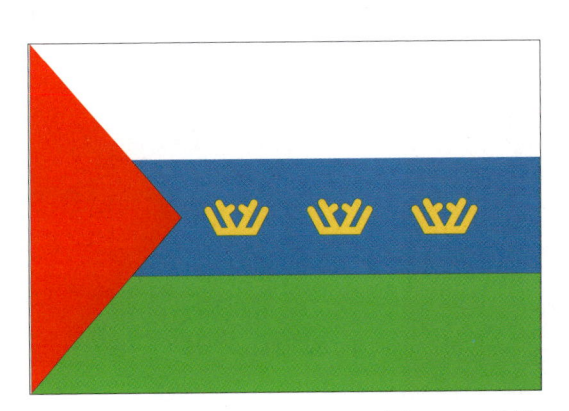

Tyumen Oblast

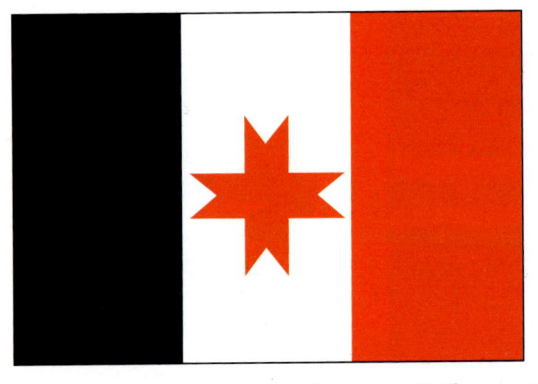

Udmurtia (Udmurt Republic)

Russian Regional Flags C-27

Current Symbols of Federal Subjects

Ulyanovsk Oblast

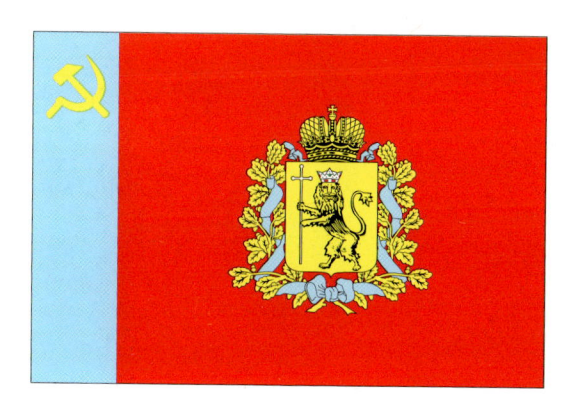

Vladimir Oblast

Volgograd Oblast

Current Symbols of Federal Subjects

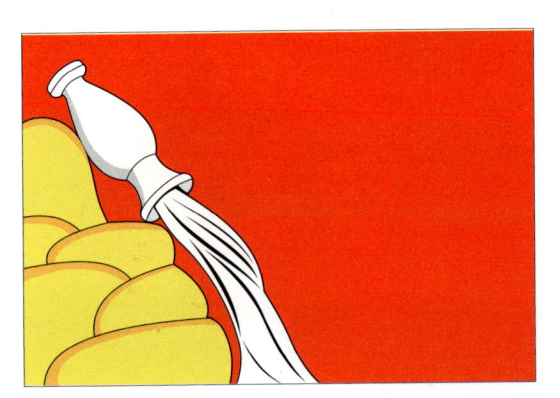

Vologda Oblast

Voronezh Oblast

Yamalo-Nenets Autonomous Okrug

Russian Regional Flags C-29

Current Symbols of Federal Subjects

Yaroslavl Oblast

Zabaikal Krai

Symbols of Merged Federal Subjects

Agin-Buryat Autonomous Okrug

C-30 *Russian Regional Flags*

Symbols of Merged Federal Subjects

Evenk Autonomous Okrug

Kamchatka Oblast

Komi-Permyak Autonomous Okrug

Russian Regional Flags   C-31

Symbols of Merged Federal Subjects

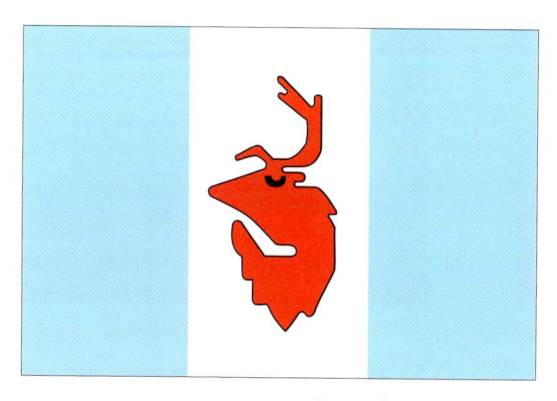

Koryak Autonomous Okrug

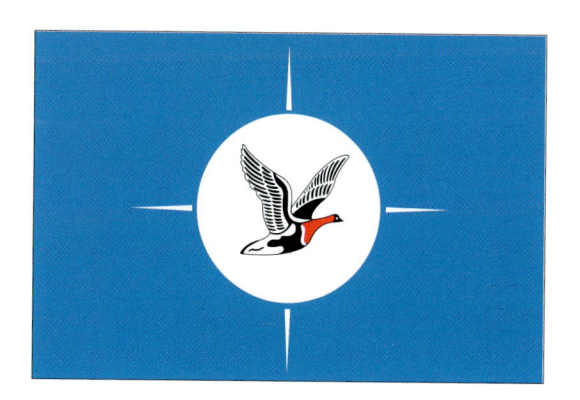

Taymyr Autonomous Okrug

Ust-Orda Buryat Autonomous Okrug

Obsolete Flags of Federal Subjects

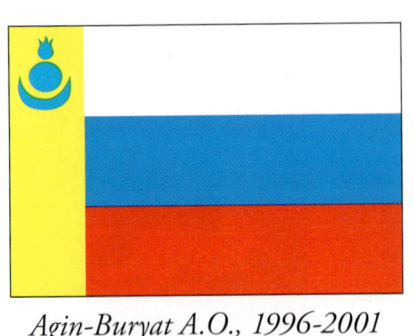

Agin-Buryat A.O., 1996-2001

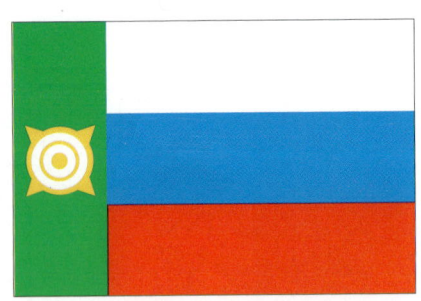

Khakassia, 1993-2002

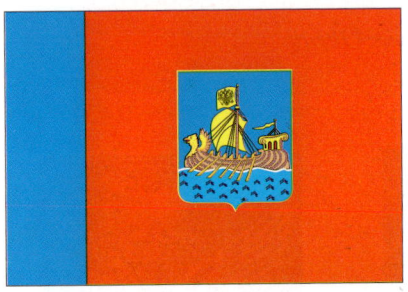

Kostroma Oblast, 2000-2006

Krasnodar Krai, 1995-2004

Mari El, 1992-2006

Sverdlovsk Oblast, 1997-2005

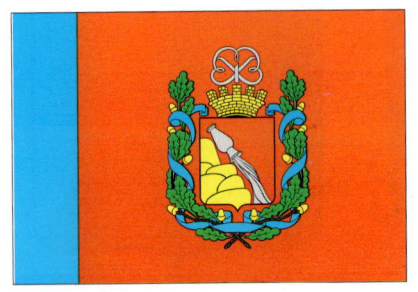

Voronezh Oblast, 1997-2005

Yaroslavl Oblast, 1998-2000

Omsk Oblast
Омская область / Omskaia oblast'

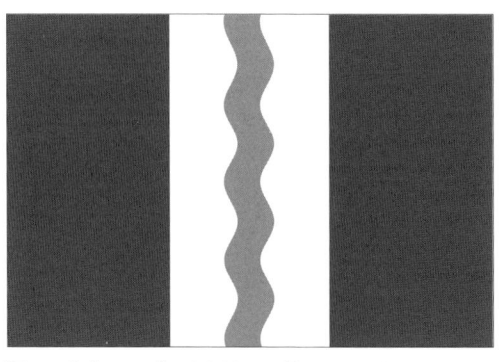

Year Adopted: 2003   **Proportions:** 2:3
Designer: unknown

Federal District: Siberian
Administrative Center: Omsk
Population: 2,014,135

Omsk Oblast's flag has three equal vertical stripes of red, white, and red. Red symbolizes bravery, courage, and fearlessness. It also stands for life, mercy, and love. White represents nobility, purity, justice, and magnanimity. It also represents the climatic features of Siberia. Centered in the white stripe is a wavy vertical blue line representing the Irtysh River, the main waterway of the oblast. Blue also symbolizes beauty, greatness, and gentleness.

Sources: Omskaia oblast', "Flag", http://www.omskportal.ru/, accessed 15 June 2008; "Flag Omskoi oblasti", *Geral'dika.ru*, http://geraldika.ru/symbols/2978, accessed 20 June 2008; "Omskaia oblast'", *Vexillographia: Flagi Rossii*, http://www.vexillographia.ru/russia/subjects/omsk.htm, accessed 1 August 2008; Borisov and Kozina, p. 240; Saprykov (2004), p. 61; Saprykov (2006), p. 61; Smetannikov, p. 72; Solov'ëv, p. 174-175; "Omsk Region (Russia)", *FOTW Flags of the World*, http://www.crwflags.com/FOTW/flags/ru-55.html, accessed 27 June 2008.

Orenburg Oblast
Оренбургская область / Orenburgskaia oblast'

Year Adopted: 1997   **Proportions:** 2:3
Designer: V. N. Eryshev

Federal District: Volga
Administrative Center: Orenburg
Population: 2,111,531

The flag of Orenburg Oblast is red with the arms of the oblast in the center. Symbols included in the arms are a running marten in blue on white, an orthodox cross and a crescent moon in gold on red, and two crossed imperial flags. The arms are topped with a gold crown. Red in the field represents historical continuity, as it has long been the color of the symbols of both Russia and the Orenburg region. The cross and the crescent moon represent the location of the oblast on the border between Europe and Asia. They also represent the two main religions of the residents—Russian Orthodoxy and Islam. The flags symbolize that Orenburg Oblast is part of the Russian Federation.

Sources: "Flag Orenburgskoi oblasti", *Geral'dika.ru*, http://geraldika.ru/symbols/1033, accessed 20 June 2008; "Orenburgskaia oblast'", *Vexillographia: Flagi Rossii*, http://www.vexillographia.ru/russia/subjects/orenburg.htm, accessed 1 August 2008; Borisov and Kozina, p. 242; Saprykov (2004), p. 62; Saprykov (2006), p. 62; Smetannikov, p. 73; Solov'ëv, p. 130-131; "Orenburg Region (Russia)", *FOTW Flags of the World*, http://www.crwflags.com/FOTW/flags/ru-56.html, accessed 27 June 2008.

Oryol Oblast
Орловская область / Orlovskaia oblast'

Year Adopted: 2002 **Proportions:** 2:3
Designer: unknown

Federal District: Central
Administrative Center: Oryol
Population: 816,895

   Oryol Oblast (or Orel Oblast) has a red flag with a light-blue stripe running along the bottom (1/5 the width of the flag). Centered in the red field are the arms of the oblast, in width 1/4 the length of the flag. Red symbolizes bravery, courage, and fearlessness. Blue represents beauty, greatness, purity of thought, and spiritual aspirations. Symbols on the arms include a two-headed Russian eagle, a fortress, stalks of grain, and an open book. The eagle represents the oblast's position as a federal subject of the Russian Federation. Below it, the fortress symbolizes the region's role in the defense of Russia, stability, dependability, and loyalty to the homeland. Grain and the green field represent agriculture and its importance in the region. The book symbolizes the literary traditions of the region.

Sources: Orlovskaia oblast', "O gerbe i flage Orlovskoi oblasti", http://www.adm.orel.ru/index.php?head=2&part=4, accessed 26, 2008; "Flag Orlovskoi oblasti", *Geral'dika.ru*, http://geraldika.ru/symbols/565, accessed 20 June 2008; "Orlovskaia oblast'", *Vexillographia: Flagi Rossii*, http://www.vexillographia.ru/russia/subjects/oryol.htm, accessed 1 August 2008; Borisov and Kozina, p. 245; Saprykov (2004), p. 63; Saprykov (2006), p. 63; Smetannikov, p. 74; Solov'ëv, p. 40-41; "Orel Region (Russia)", *FOTW Flags of the World*, http://www.crwflags.com/FOTW/flags/ru-57.html, accessed 27 June 2008.

Penza Oblast
Пензенская область / Penzenskaia oblast'

Year Adopted: 2002 **Proportions:** 1:1.6
Designer: A. N. Kniazev

Federal District: Volga
Administrative Center: Penza
Population: 1,379,839

The flag of Penza Oblast is yellow with a green vertical stripe at the hoist, approximately 1/7 the length of the flag. Centered horizontally on the flag, set slightly toward the top, is an icon known as *"Spas Nerukotvornyi"* (Our Savior Not Made by Hands). This icon style is based upon an Orthodox tradition of the first icon image—the Image of Edessa, a miraculous image of the face of Jesus on a rectangle of cloth. Yellow symbolizes fields, wisdom, knowledge, light, a rich harvest, and outlook. Green represents nature in the oblast and its forest, fertility, eternal life, and health. The icon image stands for spirituality, omniscience, and national revival.

Sources: Penzenskaia oblast', "Flag Penzenskoi oblasti", http://www.penza.ru/common/status/990, accessed 15 June 2008; "Flag Penzenskoi oblasti", *Geral'dika.ru*, http://geraldika.ru/symbols/1721, accessed 20 June 2008; "Penzenskaia oblast'", *Vexillographia: Flagi Rossii*, http://www.vexillographia.ru/russia/subjects/penza.htm, accessed 1 August 2008; Saprykov (2004), p. 64; Saprykov (2006), p. 64; Smetannikov, p. 75; Solov'ëv, p. 132-133; "Penza Region (Russia)", *FOTW Flags of the World*, http://www.crwflags.com/FOTW/flags/ru-58.html, accessed 27 June 2008; "Spas Nerukotvornyi", *Vikipediia*, no direct URL available, accessed 7 July 2008; "Image of Edessa", *Wikipedia*, http://en.wikipedia.org/wiki/Image_of_Edessa, accessed 7 July 2008.

Perm Krai
Пермский край / Permskii krai

Year Adopted: 2003; 2007   **Proportions:** 2:3
Designer: unknown

Federal District: Volga
Administrative Center: Perm
Population: 2,708,419

Perm Krai's flag has a white cross in the center, dividing the field into four rectangular panels—red at the upper hoist and lower fly, azure blue at the upper fly and lower hoist. The cross is the traditional symbol of St. George, patron saint of Russia. It is 1/4 the width and 1/6 the length of the flag. In the center of the cross are the arms of the krai, showing a bear with the Book of the Gospels on its back. The bear is shown here in white, but official descriptions of the arms have it in silver. It is meant to be a European bear, not a polar bear. The bear recalls an ancient bear cult that once existed in the region. Victory of Christianity over the pagan religion is represented by placing the Gospels on the bear's back. Above the shield is a princely crown. White, blue, and red reflect the colors of the national flag and are traditional colors of the region. White symbolizes purity and goodness, and on the flag represents peace and the purity of the thoughts of the people. Blue symbolizes beauty, gentleness, and the warmth of human relations. It also represents the open waters of the Kama River, as well as the many lakes and rivers in the region. Red is a symbol of bravery, courage, and the fearlessness of the inhabitants. The flag was initially adopted in 2003 as the flag of Perm Oblast. In 2005, Komi-Permyak Autonomous Okrug merged with Perm Oblast to form Perm Krai. The flag of the oblast continued to be used, and in 2007 that flag was formally retained for the krai.

Sources: Permskii krai, "Ofitsial'nye simvoly Permskogo kraia", http://perm.ru/region/symbols/, accessed 14 June 2008; "Flag Permskoi oblasti", *Geral'dika.ru*, http://geraldika.ru/symbols/1465, accessed 20 June 2008; "Permskii krai", *Vexillographia: Flagi Rossii*, http://www.vexillographia.ru/russia/subjects/perm.htm, accessed 1 August 2008; Borisov and Kozina, p. 251-252; Saprykov (2004), p. 65; Saprykov (2006), p. 65; Smetannikov, p. 76; "Perm Territory (Russia)", *FOTW Flags of the World*, http://www.crwflags.com/FOTW/flags/ru-59.html, accessed 27 June 2008.

Primorsky Krai
Приморский край / Primorskii krai

Year Adopted: 1995   **Proportions:** 2:3
Designer: Viktor Aleksandrovich Obertas

Federal District: Far Eastern
Administrative Center: Vladivostok
Population: 1,988,008

The flag of Primorsky Krai, or Primorye, is divided by a white diagonal stripe running from lower hoist to upper fly, meeting the corners of the flag. The stripe's width is approximately 1/5 the length of the flag. In the red panel at the hoist is a gold tiger from the arms of the region. At the lower fly, the flag is blue. Red symbolizes feats, sacrifices, victories, bravery, courage, and fearlessness. Blue represents honesty, fidelity, beauty, gentleness, and greatness. Together with white, they are the historical colors of the region and represent the territory's unity with the Russian Federation. The Siberian tiger, also referred to as the Amur or Ussuri tiger, is one of the more distinctive animals that inhabit the region and represents the natural environment of the area.

Sources: Primorskii krai, "Flag", http://www.primorsky.ru/primorye/heraldry/?a=254&s=9&p=1 and http://www.primorsky.ru/primorye/heraldry/?a=987&s=9&p=1, accessed 14 June 2008; "Flag Primorskogo kraia", *Geral'dika.ru*, http://geraldika.ru/symbols/463, accessed 18 June 2008; "Primorskii krai", *Vexillographia: Flagi Rossii*, http://www.vexillographia.ru/russia/subjects/primor.htm, accessed 1 August 2008; Borisov and Kozina, p. 82-83; Saprykov (2004), p. 34; Saprykov (2006), p. 32; Smetannikov, p. 42; Solov'ëv, p. 192-193; "Maritime Territory (Russia)", *FOTW Flags of the World*, http://www.crwflags.com/FOTW/flags/ru-25.html, accessed 27 June 2008.

Pskov Oblast
Псковская область / Pskovskaia oblast'

No flag

Federal District: Northwestern
Administrative Center: Pskov
Population: 696,392

Pskov Oblast has not adopted an official flag. At least one flag manufacturer sells an unofficial flag derived from the shield of the oblast's arms. This unofficial flag shows a yellow snow leopard on a field of blue. The leopard represents the bravery and courage of the people of Pskov, preparedness to face all enemies, and leaving no hope for any aggressors. Above the snow leopard is a bank of white clouds. A hand of blessing in gold extends down from the clouds toward the animal, strengthening its defensive functions.

Sources: Pskovskaya oblast', "Simvolika Pskovskoi oblasti", http://www.pskov.ru/ru/about_region/symbolism, accessed 15 June 2008; BIAR Natsional'naia Simvolika, "Flagi sub"ektov Rossiiskoi Federatsii", *Katalog produktsii 2007*, p 8; "Pskovskaia oblast'", *Vexillographia: Flagi Rossii*, http://www.vexillographia.ru/russia/subjects/pskov.htm, accessed 1 August 2008; Borisov and Kozina, p. 258-259; Saprykov (2004), p. 66; Saprykov (2006), p. 66; Smetannikov, p. 77.

Rostov Oblast
Ростовская область / Rostovskaia oblast'

Year Adopted: 1996 **Proportions:** 2:3
Designer: unknown

Federal District: Southern
Administrative Center: Rostov-on-Don
Population: 4,241,821

There are four stripes on the flag of Rostov Oblast—one vertical white stripe running along the hoist, and three equal horizontal stripes, of blue, yellow and red, running to the fly. The white stripe is 1/5 of the length of the flag. This design derives from a flag dating to 1918. On that flag blue symbolized the Don Cossacks, yellow the Kalmuks, and red the Russians (although yellow is now said to represent all people living along the river). The white stripe was added as a symbol of unity with the Russian Federation.

Sources: Rostovskaia oblast', "Flag Rostovskoi oblasti", http://www.donland.ru/content/info.asp?partId=4&infoId=671&topicFolderId=90&topicInfoId=0, accessed 15 June 2008; "Flag Rostovskoi oblasti", *Geral'dika.ru*, http://geraldika.ru/symbols/1052, accessed 20 June 2008; "Rostovskaia oblast'", *Vexillographia: Flagi Rossii*, http://www.vexillographia.ru/russia/subjects/rostov.htm, accessed 1 August 2008; Borisov and Kozina, p. 262; Saprykov (2004), p. 67; Saprykov (2006), p. 67; Smetannikov, p. 78; Solov'ëv, p. 106-107; "Rostov Region (Russia)", *FOTW Flags of the World*, http://www.crwflags.com/FOTW/flags/ru-61.html, accessed 27 June 2008.

Ryazan Oblast
Рязанская область / Riazanskaia oblast'

Year Adopted: 2000 **Proportions:** 2:3
Designer: Mikhail K. Shelkovenko

Federal District: Central
Administrative Center: Ryazan
Population: 1,157,740

Ryazan Oblast has a flag with three horizontal stripes of white, yellow, and red in proportions of 1:2:1. Centered in the yellow stripe is an image of a prince from the arms of the oblast. The armed prince represents the role of the region in the defense of Russia. White on the flag is reminiscent of an ancient emblem of the region—a white horse. The yellow comes from the company standards of regiments from the region used as early as the reign of Peter I. Red recalls the military ribbons of those regiments.

Sources: Riazanskaia oblast', "Ofitsial'naia simvolika", http://www.ryazanreg.ru/ryazan/symbolism/, accessed 15 June 2008; "Flag Riazanskoi oblasti", *Geral'dika.ru*, http://geraldika.ru/symbols/665, accessed 20 June 2008; "Riazanskaia oblast'", *Vexillographia: Flagi Rossii*, http://www.vexillographia.ru/russia/subjects/ryazan.htm, accessed 1 August 2008; Borisov and Kozina, p. 269; Saprykov (2004), p. 68; Saprykov (2006), p. 68; Smetannikov, p. 79; Solov'ëv, p. 42-43; "Ryazan' Region (Russia)", *FOTW Flags of the World*, http://www.crwflags.com/FOTW/flags/ru-rya.html, accessed 27 June 2008.

St. Petersburg (city)
Санкт-Петербург / Sankt-Peterburg

Year Adopted: 1992   **Proportions:** 2:3
Designer: unknown

Federal District: Northwestern
Population: 4,581,854

St. Petersburg bases its flag on the shield of the city's arms. On a field of red, two white anchors are crossed—one for use on the river and the other for use at sea. The anchors represent the location of the city on the Neva River and its importance as a port on the Baltic Sea. In front of the anchors is a gold scepter topped by a two-headed eagle. It symbolizes royal authority and the historical status of St. Petersburg as the imperial capital from 1713 to 1918. The current design of the arms is based upon one used in Imperial Russia. Red on the flag recalls the blood spilled at the site during the Great Northern War with Sweden (1700-21) when Russia first gained control of this region on the Baltic Sea.

Sources: Sankt-Peterburg, "Ofitsial'nye simvoly Sankt-Peterburga", http://www.gov.spb.ru/gov/admin/gerb, accessed 15 June 2008; "Flag goroda Sankt-Peterburg", *Geral'dika.ru*, http://geraldika.ru/symbols/518, accessed 18 June 2008; "Gorod Sankt-Peterburg", *Vexillographia: Flagi Rossii*, http://www.vexillographia.ru/russia/subjects/st_peter.htm, accessed 1 August 2008; Borisov and Kozina, p. 388; Saprykov (2004), p. 84; Saprykov (2006), p. 84; Smetannikov, p. 95; Solov'ëv, p. 76-77; Saint Petersburg (Russia), *FOTW Flags of the World*, http://www.crwflags.com/FOTW/flags/ru-spe.html, accessed 27 June 2008.

Sakha Republic (Yakutia)
Республика Саха (Якутия) / Respublika Sakha (Iakutiia)

Year Adopted: 1992   **Proportions:** 1:2
Designers: L. D. Sleptsova, M. G. Starostin, and A. P. Zakharova

Federal District: Far Eastern
Capital: Yakutsk
Population: 949,753

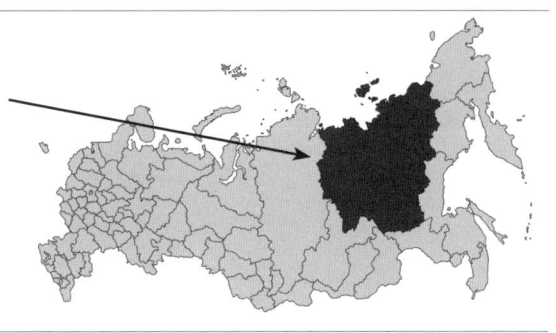

The flag of Sakha (Yakutia) has a field of light blue. Running horizontally at the base are narrow stripes of white, red, and green, 1/16, 1/16, and 1/8 the width of the flag. Centered in the blue is a white solar disk with a diameter of roughly 1/5 the width of the flag. Blue symbolizes the clear, peaceful northern sky, hope, and freedom. White is the color of snow and represents the severe beauty of the northern region, the extreme conditions of the people's lives, and the purity of their thoughts and temperaments. Red symbolizes vitality, beauty, loyalty to the native land, and progress. Green represents the short, bright summer, and the open spaces of the taiga. It also symbolizes revival, friendship, brotherhood, and the Turkic origins of the people of Sakha. The white sun comes from the mythology of the Yakut people who consider themselves "children of the white sun".

Sources: Respublika Sakha (Iakutiia), "Gosudarstvennyi flag Respubliki Sakha (Iakutiia)", http://www.sakha.gov.ru/main.asp?c=1552, accessed 14 June 2008; "Flag Respubliki Sakha (Iakutiya)", Geral'dika.ru, http://geraldika.ru/symbols/293, accessed 17 June 2008; "Sakha (Iakutiia)", Vexillographia: Flagi Rossii, http://www.vexillographia.ru/russia/subjects/saha.htm, accessed 1 August 2008; Borisov and Kozina, p. 47; Saprykov (2004), p. 24; Saprykov (2006), p. 21; Sharkov, p. 66-68, 159-162; Smetannikov, p. 31; Solov'ëv, p. 190-191; "Yakutia (Russia)", FOTW Flags of the World, http://www.crwflags.com/FOTW/flags/ru-14.html, accessed 27 June 2008.

Sakhalin Oblast
Сахалинская область / Sakhalinskaia oblast'

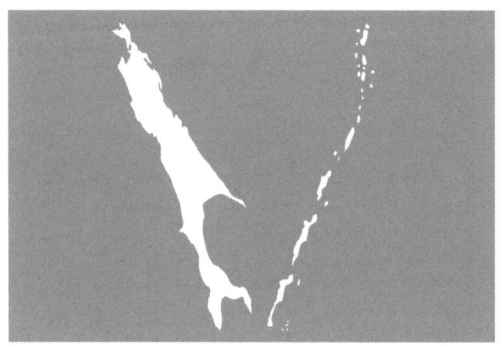

Year Adopted: 1997 **Proportions:** 2:3
Designer: Vitalii Evgen'evich Gomelevskii

Federal District: Far Eastern
Administrative Center:
 Yuzhno-Sakhalinsk
Population: 514,520

The flag of Sakhalin Oblast is blue with an emerald-green hue. This color is reminiscent of a sea wave and represents the importance of the ocean to the region. Centered on the flag is a cartographic image of Sakhalin Island and the Kuril archipelago in white. The image of the islands represents the historical, natural, and geographic distinctiveness of the region, as well as its position as an integral part of Russia. White is a traditional color representing the expanse of Siberia, and symbolizes the concepts of purity, good, and independence.

Sources: Sakhalinskaia oblast', "Simvolika", http://www.adm.sakhalin.ru/index.php?id=79, and "Zakon Sakhalinskoi oblasti o flage Sakhalinskoi oblasti - sub"ekta Rossiiskoi Federasii", http://www.adm.sakhalin.ru/index.php?id=83, accessed 15 June 2008; "Flag Sakhalinskoi oblasti", *Geral'dika.ru*, http://geraldika.ru/symbols/810, accessed 20 June 2008; "Sakhalinskaia oblast'", *Vexillographia: Flagi Rossii*, http://www.vexillographia.ru/russia/subjects/sahalin.htm, accessed 1 August 2008; Borisov and Kozina, p. 290; Saprykov (2004), p. 71; Saprykov (2006), p. 71; Smetannikov, p. 82; Solov'ëv, p. 202-203; "Sakhalin Region (Russia)", *FOTW Flags of the World*, http://www.crwflags.com/FOTW/flags/ru-sak.html, accessed 27 June 2008.

Samara Oblast
Самарская область / Samarskaia oblast'

Year Adopted: 1998   **Proportions:** 2:3
Designer: unknown

Federal District: Volga
Administrative Center: Samara
Population: 3,171,446

The flag of Samara Oblast consists of three equal horizontal stripes of red, white, and blue with the arms of the oblast in the center, more than half the width of the flag high. Red represents courage, boldness, magnanimity, and love. White symbolizes nobility and frankness. Blue is associated with fidelity, honesty, faultlessness, and chastity. The main symbol in the arms is a white billy goat on a light blue field, symbolizing unwavering strength and the honorable quality of leadership. Stripes on the flag are reminiscent of the "Samara banner", a flag presented by the people of Samara to Bulgarian volunteers during the Russo-Turkish War of 1877-78. During the Battle of Stara Zagora, the Bulgarians heroically prevented the Ottomans from capturing the banner.

Sources: Samarskaia oblast', "Flag Samarskoi oblasti", http://www.adm.samara.ru/oblast/oblast_simvolika/1131/, accessed 15 June 2008; "Flag Samarskoi oblasti", *Geral'dika.ru*, http://geraldika.ru/symbols/1078, accessed 20 June 2008; "Samarskaia oblast'", *Vexillographia: Flagi Rossii*, http://www.vexillographia.ru/russia/subjects/samara.htm, accessed 1 August 2008; Borisov and Kozina, p. 277; Saprykov (2004), p. 69; Saprykov (2006), p. 69; Smetannikov, p. 80; Solov'ëv, p. 134-135; "Samara Region (Russia)", *FOTW Flags of the World*, http://www.crwflags.com/FOTW/flags/ru-sam.html, accessed 27 June 2008; "Samara flag", *Wikipedia*, http://en.wikipedia.org/wiki/Samara_banner, accessed 30 September 2009.

Saratov Oblast
Саратовская область / Saratovskaia oblast'

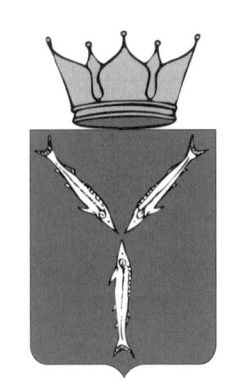

Year Adopted: 1996 **Proportions:** 2:3
Designer: V. V. Volodin

Federal District: Volga
Administrative Center: Saratov
Population: 2,572,866

Saratov Oblast's flag has a white field with a red stripe along the bottom, 1/3 of the hoist height. White on the flag symbolizes purity of thoughts, nobility of deeds, truthfulness, and the lofty spirituality of those living in the region. Red represents courage, boldness, fearlessness, magnanimity, and love. Centered in the white field are the arms of the oblast surrounded by a wreath of oak and laurel branches. The arms are 1/4 the length of the flag. On the shield are three sterlets, a species of sturgeon, in white on a blue field, representing the importance of the fishing industry to the region.

Sources: Saratovskaia oblast', "Gosudarstvennaia simvolika", http://saratov.gov.ru/region/emblem.php, accessed 15 June 2008; "Flag Saratovskoi oblasti", *Geral'dika.ru*, http://geraldika.ru/symbols/131, accessed 20 June 2008; "Saratovskaia oblast'", *Vexillographia: Flagi Rossii*, http://www.vexillographia.ru/russia/subjects/saratov.htm, accessed 1 August 2008; Borisov and Kozina, p. 282; Saprykov (2004), p. 70; Saprykov (2006), p. 70; Smetannikov, p. 81; Solov'ëv, p. 136-137; "Saratov Region (Russia)", *FOTW Flags of the World*, http://www.crwflags.com/FOTW/flags/ru-64.html, accessed 27 June 2008.

Smolensk Oblast
Смоленская область / Smolenskaia oblast'

Year Adopted: 1998 **Proportions:** 2:3
Designer: Gennadii Vladimirovich Razhnëv

Federal District: Central
Administrative Center: Smolensk
Population: 974,139

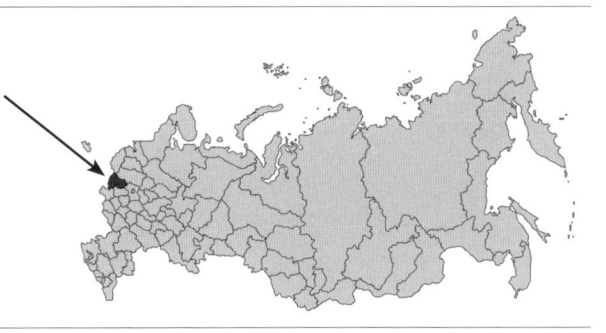

The flag of Smolensk Oblast is red with two narrow horizontal yellow stripes in the lower half, creating three red stripes. In the upper hoist are the arms of the oblast. Red is a symbol of the historical status of Smolensk as a battleground in some of the most significant wars in Russian history. The first red stripe stands for the war against the Polish interventionists (1609-11), the second for the French invasion of 1812, and the third for World War II. Yellow stripes on red also recall the Order of Lenin awarded to the region in recognition of its valor during World War II. In addition, yellow represents two mythical birds—the *gamayun* and the phoenix. The *gamayun* (shown perched on a gun carriage in the arms on a white field) is a traditional symbol of wisdom and knowledge. In the arms of Smolensk Oblast, it also represents peace, happiness, wealth, and prosperity. Allusion to the phoenix recognizes that Smolensk has twice risen from the ashes of war to rebuild (after the Napoleonic War and World War II). The gun carriage represents might and impenetrability, as well as mercilessness and retribution toward the enemies of Russia. On the arms, the crown symbolizes that Smolensk is an integral part of the Russian Federation.

Sources: Smolenskaia oblast', "Ofitsial'nye simvoly Smolenskoi oblasti", http://admin.smolensk.ru/of_sim_smol.htm and http://admin.smolensk.ru/of_sim1.htm, accessed 15 June 2008; "Flag Smolenskoi oblasti", *Geral'dika*.ru, http://geraldika.ru/symbols/1123, accessed 20 June 2008; "Smolenskaia oblast'", *Vexillographia: Flagi Rossii*, http://www.vexillographia.ru/russia/subjects/smolensk.htm, accessed 1 August 2008; Borisov and Kozina, p. 306; Saprykov (2004), p. 73; Saprykov (2006), p. 73; Smetannikov, p. 84; Solov'ëv, p. 44-45; "Smolensk Region (Russia)", *FOTW Flags of the World*, http://www.crwflags.com/FOTW/flags/ru-67.html, accessed 27 June 2008; "Gamayun", *Vikipediia*, no direct URL available, accessed 9 July 2008; "Gamayun", *Wikipedia*, http://en.wikipedia.org/wiki/Gamayun, accessed 9 July 2008.

Stavropol Krai
Ставропольский край / Stavropol'skii krai

Year Adopted: 1997   **Proportions:** 2:3
Designers: Vadim Nikolaevich Solov'ëv, Tat'iana Petrovna Solov'ëva, and Irina Nikolaevna Postnikova

Federal District: Southern
Administrative Center: Stavropol
Population: 2,707,290

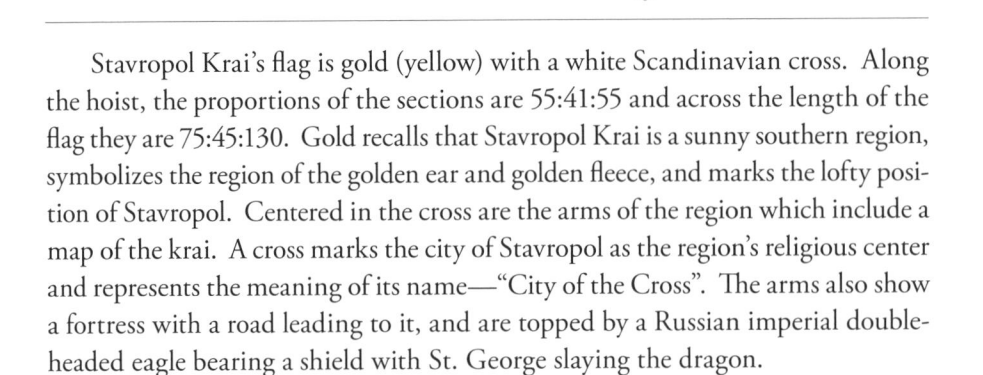

Stavropol Krai's flag is gold (yellow) with a white Scandinavian cross. Along the hoist, the proportions of the sections are 55:41:55 and across the length of the flag they are 75:45:130. Gold recalls that Stavropol Krai is a sunny southern region, symbolizes the region of the golden ear and golden fleece, and marks the lofty position of Stavropol. Centered in the cross are the arms of the region which include a map of the krai. A cross marks the city of Stavropol as the region's religious center and represents the meaning of its name—"City of the Cross". The arms also show a fortress with a road leading to it, and are topped by a Russian imperial double-headed eagle bearing a shield with St. George slaying the dragon.

Sources: Stavropol'skii krai, "Flag Stavropol'skogo kraia", http://www.govsk.ru/o_stavropolskom_krae/gerald/flag/, accessed 14 June 2008 "Flag Stavropol'skogo kraia", *Geral'dika.ru*, http://geraldika.ru/symbols/455, accessed 18 June 2008; "Stavropol'skii krai", *Vexillographia: Flagi Rossii*, http://www.vexillographia.ru/russia/subjects/stavrpol.htm, accessed 1 August 2008; Borisov and Kozina, p. 86; Saprykov (2004), p. 35; Saprykov (2006), p. 33; Smetannikov, p. 43; Solov'ëv, p. 100-101; "Stavropol Territory (Russia)", *FOTW Flags of the World*, http://www.crwflags.com/FOTW/flags/ru-26.html, accessed 27 June 2008.

Sverdlovsk Oblast
Свердловская область / Sverdlovskaia oblast'

Year Adopted: 2005   **Proportions:** 2:3
Designers: A. N. Vybornov, V. V. Startsev, and O. V. Startseva

Federal District: Urals
Administrative Center:
 Yekaterinburg
Population: 4,394,649

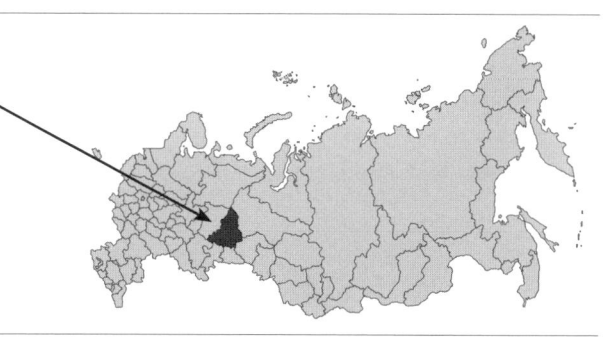

Sverdlovsk Oblast has a flag with horizontal stripes of varying width and color, from top to bottom: white, blue, white, and green, in proportions of 7:9:1:3. White is the color of purity, innocence, and peace. Blue represents loyalty, honor, glory, and sincerity. Green symbolizes life, health, renewal, and the natural riches of the Urals.

Another design, used 1997-2005, included the arms of the oblast centered on the top two stripes. In 2005, the arms were revised and dropped from the flag design.

Sources: Sverdlovskaia oblast', "Simvolika Sverdlovskoi oblasti", http://www.midural.ru/midural-new/page_oblast14.htm, accessed 15 June 2008; "Flag Sverdlovskoi oblasti (2005 g.)", *Geral'dika.ru*, http://geraldika.ru/symbols/11356, accessed 20 June 2008; "Flag Sverdlovskoi oblasti (1997 g.)", *Geral'dika.ru*, http://geraldika.ru/symbols/623, accessed 7 August 2008; "Sverdlovskaia oblast'", *Vexillographia: Flagi Rossii*, http://www.vexillographia.ru/russia/subjects/sverdlov.htm, accessed 1 August 2008; Borisov and Kozina, p. 294; Saprykov (2004), p. 72; Saprykov (2006), p. 72; Smetannikov, p. 83; Solov'ëv, p. 144-145; "Sverdlovsk Region (Russia)", *FOTW Flags of the World*, http://www.crwflags.com/FOTW/flags/ru-66.html, accessed 27 June 2008.

Tambov Oblast
Тамбовская область / Tambovskaia oblast'

Year Adopted: 2005 **Proportions:** 2:3
Designer: unknown

Federal District: Central
Administrative Center: Tambov
Population: 1,096,879

    Tambov Oblast's flag is divided vertically into two equal parts—red at the hoist and blue at the fly. Red is a symbol of courage and steadfastness. It reflects the bravery of the inhabitants, their magnanimity, their aspirations to unity and solidarity, and the continuity of the generations. Red is also drawn from historical flags of Russia, emblems of the Tambov area, and from the flags of the Soviet period. Blue symbolizes the greatness, natural beauty, and cleanliness of the Tambov region, faithfulness to its traditions, faultlessness, and well-being. Centered on the flag are the arms of the oblast, which show a beehive and three bees in white on a blue field. The beehive symbolizes the concept of home, and the bees represent industriousness and thrift. Topping the arms is a gold crown. The width of the arms is roughly 1/3 the length of the flag.

Sources: Tambovskaia oblast', "Simvolika oblasti", http://www.tambov.gov.ru//?Page=171, accessed 15 June 2008; Tambovskaia oblast', "Zakon o flage Tambovskoi oblasti", http://www.regadm.tambov.ru/flag.htm, accessed 9 July 2008; "Flag Tambovskoi oblasti", *Geral'dika.ru*, http://geraldika.ru/symbols/11007, accessed 20 June 2008; "Tambovskaia oblast'", *Vexillographia: Flagi Rossii*, http://www.vexillographia.ru/russia/subjects/tambov.htm, accessed 1 August 2008; Borisov and Kozina, p. 311; Saprykov (2004), p. 74; Saprykov (2006), p. 74; Smetannikov, p. 85; "Tambov Region (Russia)", *FOTW Flags of the World*, http://www.crwflags.com/FOTW/flags/ru-68.html, accessed 27 June 2008.

Tatarstan, Republic of
Республика Татарстан / Respublika Tatarstan

Year Adopted: 1991   **Proportions:** 1:2
Designer: T. G. Khaziakhmetov

Federal District: Volga
Capital: Kazan
Population: 3,768,580

Three horizontal stripes make up the flag of Tatarstan—green, white, and red in proportions of 7:1:7. Green symbolizes the color of spring and revival, white is the color of purity, and red stands for maturity, energy, strength, and life.

Sources: Respublika Tatarstan, "Gosudarstvennaia simvolika," http://www.tatar.ru/index.php?DNSID=74514c0fbf32e 262abafda13efc95e1b&node_id=21, accessed 14 June 2008; "Flag Respubliki Tatarstan", *Geral'dika.ru*, http://geraldika. ru/symbols/363, accessed 17 June 2008; "Tatarstan", *Vexillographia: Flagi Rossii*, http://www.vexillographia.ru/russia/ subjects/tataria.htm, accessed 1 August 2008; Borisov and Kozina, p. 52; Saprykov (2004), p. 26; Saprykov (2006), p. 23; Sharkov, p. 73-77, 167-171; Smetannikov, p. 33; Solov'ëv, p. 116-117; "Tataria (Russia)", *FOTW Flags of the World*, http://www.crwflags.com/FOTW/flags/ru-16.html, accessed 27 June 2008.

Tomsk Oblast
Томская область / Tomskaia oblast'

Year Adopted: 1997 **Proportions:** 2:3
Designer: A. Iu. Akimov

Federal District: Siberian
Administrative Center: Tomsk
Population: 1,038,508

The flag of Tomsk Oblast is white with the arms in the center. On the shield is an image of a leaping white horse on a green field. The horse represents the importance of horses in Tatar culture, and the region's significance as a trade route and horse-breeding center. White is the color of nobility and frankness. Green in the arms symbolizes hope, abundance, freedom, and joy. A crown tops the shield.

Sources: Tomskaia oblast', "Simvolika Tomska", http://tomck.com/gerb.php, accessed 15 June 2008; "Flag Tomskoi oblasti", *Geral'dika.ru*, http://geraldika.ru/symbols/1145, accessed 20 June 2008; "Tomskaia oblast'", *Vexillographia: Flagi Rossii*, http://www.vexillographia.ru/russia/subjects/tomsk.htm, accessed 1 August 2008; Borisov and Kozina, p. 321; Saprykov (2004), p. 76; Saprykov (2006), p. 76; Smetannikov, p. 87; Solov'ëv, p. 176-177; "Tomsk Region (Russia)", *FOTW Flags of the World*, http://www.crwflags.com/FOTW/flags/ru-70.html, accessed 27 June 2008.

Tula Oblast
Тульская область / Tul'skaia oblast'

Year Adopted: 2005   **Proportions:** 2:3
Designer: unknown

Federal District: Central
Administrative Center: Tula
Population: 1,553,145

    Tula Oblast's flag is an armorial banner, drawn directly from the shield of the arms. It is red with two gold hammers and three silver sword blades (without handles or hilts). The swords are crossed, with one horizontal and the other two at diagonals; the hammers are above and below the swords, framed by the diagonally-oriented blades. Each sword is nearly the width of the flag. The city of Tula has been an important center for the manufacture of armaments since the early 1700s.

Sources: Tul'skaia oblast', "Gerb, flag Tul'skoi oblasti", http://www.admportal.tula.ru/catalog/229.aspx, accessed 15 June 2008; "Flag Tyl'skoi oblasti", *Geral'dika.ru*, http://geraldika.ru/symbols/13487, accessed 20 June 2008; "Tul'skaia oblast'", *Vexillographia: Flagi Rossii*, http://www.vexillographia.ru/russia/subjects/tula.htm, accessed 1 August 2008; Borisov and Kozina, p. 322-323; Saprykov (2004), p. 77; Saprykov (2006), p. 77; Smetannikov, p. 88; "Tula Region (Russia)", *FOTW Flags of the World*, http://www.crwflags.com/FOTW/flags/ru-71.html, accessed 27 June 2008.

Tuva (Tyva) Republic
Республика Тыва / Respublika Tyva

Year Adopted: 1992   **Proportions:** 2:3; changed from 1:2 in 2002
Designers: Ivan Chamvoevich Salchak and Oleg Il'ich Lazeev

Federal District: Siberian
Capital: Kyzyl
Population: 313,940

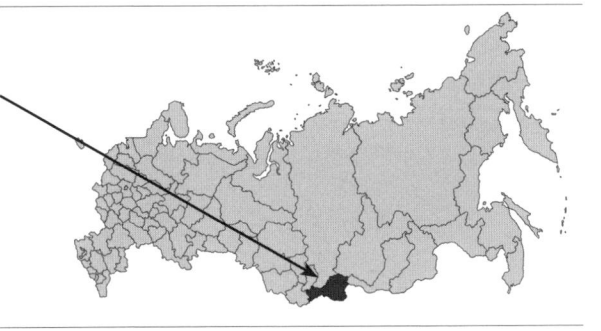

Tuva's flag has a gold triangle at the hoist. In the center of the flag is a sideways "Y" shape in blue, with its base toward the fly, separated by white fimbriations from the hoist triangle and the blue field. The resulting stripes represent the Greater Yenisei (Bii-Khem) and Lesser Yenisei (Kaa-Khem) rivers which join near the capital city of Kyzyl to form the Upper Yenisei (Ulug-Khem) river. Gold stands for riches, leadership, and greatness. White represents purity and the nobility of public morals. It is also reminiscent of tea with milk—the traditional drink which Tuvans present first to visitors in their homes. Blue is the color of the clean sky, and symbolizes the loftiness of purposes, mutual respect, and harmony in society.

Sources: Respublika Tyva, "Gosudarstvennaia simvolika i gimn", http://gov.tuva.ru/index.php?do=static&page=gossimvol, accessed 23 June 2008; "Flag Respubliki Tyva", *Geral'dika.ru*, http://geraldika.ru/symbols/379, accessed 17 June 2008; "Respublika Tyva", *Vexillographia: Flagi Rossii*, http://www.vexillographia.ru/russia/subjects/tuva.htm, accessed 1 August 2008; Borisov and Kozina, p. 56; Saprykov (2004), p. 27; Saprykov (2006), p. 24; Sharkov, p. 78-80, 172-174; Smetannikov, p. 34; Solov'ëv, p. 160-161; "Tuva (Russia)", *FOTW Flags of the World*, http://www.crwflags.com/FOTW/flags/ru-ty.html, accessed 27 June 2008.

Tver Oblast
Тверская область / Tverskaia oblast'

Year Adopted: 1996　　**Proportions:** 2:3
Designer: V. I. Lavrenov

Federal District: Central
Administrative Center: Tver
Population: 1,369,413

The flag of Tver Oblast is divided into three vertical stripes of yellow-red-yellow in proportions of 1:2:1. Yellow (gold) recalls the color of the standard of the princes of Tver. The center stripe is red—the traditional color of the Rus. In the center of the flag is an element from the arms of the oblast. The emblem shows a gold throne (also called a "princely chair"), with "Monomakh's cap" sitting on a green cushion. This crown is a traditional symbol of the Russian monarchy and was used until the time of Peter the Great. It is a gold filigree skullcap with sable trim, decorated with pearls and gems.

Sources: Tverskaia oblast', "Gerb i flag Tverskoi oblasti", http://www.zsto.ru/o_tverskoj_oblasti/state_emblems/index.html, accessed 15 June 2008; "Flag Tverskoi oblasti", *Geral'dika.ru*, http://geraldika.ru/symbols/1137, accessed 20 June 2008; "Tverskaia oblast'", *Vexillographia: Flagi Rossii*, http://www.vexillographia.ru/russia/subjects/tver.htm, accessed 1 August 2008; Borisov and Kozina, p. 313; Saprykov (2004), p. 75; Saprykov (2006), p. 75; Smetannikov, p. 86; Solov'ëv, p. 48-49; "Tver Region (Russia)", *FOTW Flags of the World*, http://www.crwflags.com/FOTW/flags/ru-69.html, accessed 27 June 2008; "Shapka Monomakha", *Vikipediia*, no direct URL available, accessed 9 July 2008; "Monomakh's Cap", *Wikipedia*, http://en.wikipedia.org/wiki/Monomakh%27s_Cap, accessed 9 July 2008.

Tyumen Oblast
Тюменская область / Tiumenskaia oblast'

Year Adopted: 1995, 2008 **Proportions:** 2:3
Designers: A. V. Neskorov, S. A. Zdanovskii, and V. A. Tregubov

Federal District: Urals
Administrative Center: Tyumen
Population: 3,398,921

Tyumen Oblast's flag has three equal horizontal stripes and a triangle at the hoist. The triangle is red and the stripes are white over blue over green. Red is the color of life, strength, beauty, brotherhood, and unity. White symbolizes peace, purity, truth, and perfection. Blue represents the sky (or heaven) and lofty ideals. Green symbolizes renewal, hope, and youth. In addition, white stands for snow, blue for rivers and lakes, and green for the forest. On the blue stripe are three stylized crowns fashioned from elements of the traditional ornaments of the northern people, reminiscent of the antlers of a reindeer. The crowns resemble those in the arms of the oblast except that they are gold, symbolizing wealth and wisdom. Three crowns represent Tyumen Oblast and the two autonomous okrugs which are included in the oblast's territory—Khanty-Mansi A.O. and Yamalo-Nenets A.O.

An earlier flag, used from 1995 to 2008, was exactly the same except that the crown nearest the hoist triangle was silver with a gold outline. In that flag, the silver crown represented Tyumen Oblast and the gold crowns represented the autonomous okrugs.

Sources: Tiumenskaia oblast', "Simvolika Tiumenskoi oblasti", http://www.admtyumen.ru/ogv_ru/about/simbolism.htm, accessed 16 September 2009; "Flag Tiumenskoi oblasti", *Geral'dika.ru*, http://geraldika.ru/symbols/21968, accessed 16 September 2009; "Flag Tiumenskoi oblasti", *Geral'dika.ru*, http://geraldika.ru/symbols/1172, accessed 20 June 2008; "Tiumenskaia oblast'", *Vexillographia: Flagi Rossii*, http://www.vexillographia.ru/russia/subjects/tyumen.htm, accessed 1 August 2008; Borisov and Kozina, p. 327; Saprykov (2004), p. 78; Saprykov (2006), p. 78; Smetannikov, p. 89; Solov'ëv, p. 146-147; "Tyumen Region (Russia)", *FOTW Flags of the World*, http://www.crwflags.com/FOTW/flags/ru-72.html, accessed 27 June 2008.

Udmurtia (Udmurt Republic)
Удмуртская Республика / Udmurtskaia Respublika

Year Adopted: 1993   **Proportions:** 1:2
Designer: Iurii Nikolaevich Lobanov

Federal District: Volga
Capital: Izhevsk
Population: 1,528,488

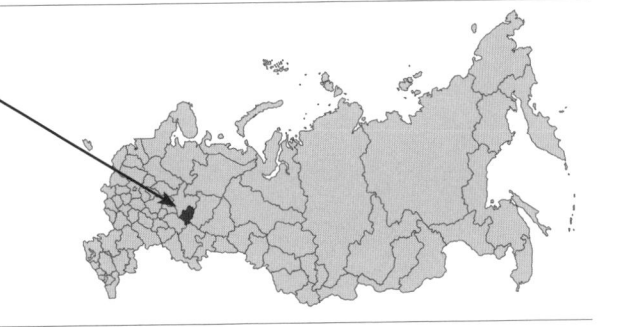

Udmurtia's flag consists of three equal vertical stripes—black, white, and red. In the center of the white stripe is a red solar sign with eight points (5/6 the width of the stripe). Black represents the land and stability, red is the color of the sun and symbolizes life, and white stands for the cosmos and the purity of moral principles. According to legend, the sun symbol protects a person against misfortune.

Sources: Udmurtskaia Respublika, "Gosudarstvennyi flag Udmurtskoi Respubliki", http://www.udmurt.ru/ru/official/gos_symbol/flag/flag.php, accessed 14 June 2008; "Flag Udmurtskoi Respubliki", *Geral'dika.ru*, http://geraldika.ru/symbols/391, accessed 17 June 2008; "Udmurtiia", *Vexillographia: Flagi Rossii*, http://www.vexillographia.ru/russia/subjects/udmurtia.htm, accessed 1 August 2008; Borisov and Kozina, p. 57; Saprykov (2004), p. 28; Saprykov (2006), p. 25; Sharkov, p. 81-87, 175-180; Smetannikov, p. 35; Solov'ëv, p. 118-119; "Udmurtia (Russia)", *FOTW Flags of the World*, http://www.crwflags.com/FOTW/flags/ru-ud.html, accessed 27 June 2008.

Ulyanovsk Oblast
Ульяновская область / Ul'ianovskaia oblast'

Year Adopted: 2004   **Proportions:** 2:3
Designer: Nikolai Sergeev

Federal District: Volga
Administrative Center:
  Ulyanovsk
Population: 1,304,990

Reminiscent of the Russian national flag, Ulyanovsk Oblast's flag can be considered to have three stripes of white, blue, and red. Unlike the national flag, the white stripe constitutes the major field of the flag, 2/3 the height of the hoist. The blue and red stripes are each 1/6 of the height of the hoist. At its top the blue stripe has waves, separated from the white by fimbriations of white and blue. The bottom stripe is red. White symbolizes purity, nobility, and peace. Blue represents the water of the Volga River. Red stands for the rich history of the region. Centered on the white stripe are the arms of the oblast which show a column in silver. Two lions are supporters, and a crown tops the arms.

Sources: "Flag Iul'ianovskoi oblasti (2004 g,)", *Geral'dika.ru*, http://geraldika.ru/symbols/2202, accessed 20 June 2008; "Iul'ianovskaia oblast'", *Vexillographia: Flagi Rossii,* http://www.vexillographia.ru/russia/subjects/ulianov.htm, accessed 1 August 2008; Borisov and Kozina, p. 329; Saprykov (2004), p. 79; Saprykov (2006), p. 79; Smetannikov, p. 90; Solov'ëv, p. 138-139; "Ulyanovsk region (Russia)", *FOTW Flags of the World,* http://www.crwflags.com/FOTW/flags/ru-73.html, accessed 27 June 2008.

Vladimir Oblast
Владимирская область / Vladimirskaia oblast'

Year Adopted: 1999 **Proportions:** 1:2
Designer: unknown

Federal District: Central
Administrative Center: Vladimir
Population: 1,439,761

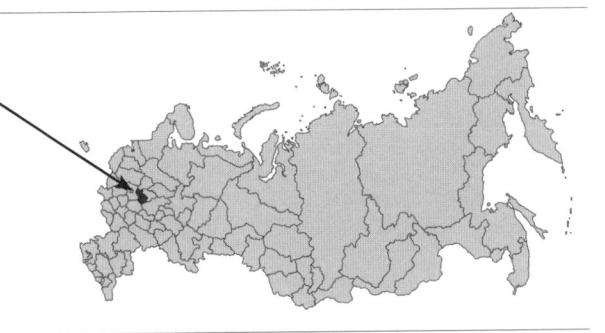

The flag of Vladimir Oblast is red with a blue stripe at the hoist, 1/8 the length of the flag. Red on the flag symbolizes courage and bravery. The red and blue recall the flag of the Russian SFSR. At the upper hoist on the blue stripe is a gold hammer and sickle, symbols also drawn from that flag. Centered on the red field, about 1/3 the length of the flag, are the arms of the oblast in gold. The central figure of the arms is a golden lion, a symbol of strength, courage, and magnanimity. He is holding a tall silver cross representing the religion of the inhabitants, and wears a crown. A crown also tops the shield, which is surrounded by a wreath of oak leaves wrapped in a ribbon of St. Andrew.

Sources: Vladimirskaia oblast', "O flage Vladimirskoi oblasti", http://avo.ru/index.php?option=com_content&task=view&id=29&Itemid=35, accessed 14 June 2008; "Flag Vladimirskoi oblasti", *Geral'dika.ru*, http://geraldika.ru/symbols/656, accessed 19 June 2008; "Vladimirskaia oblast'", *Vexillographia: Flagi Rossii*, http://www.vexillographia.ru/russia/subjects/vladimir.htm, accessed 1 August 2008; Borisov and Kozina, p. 113; Saprykov (2004), p. 41; Saprykov (2006), p. 40; Smetannikov, p. 50; Solov'ëv, p. 24-25; "Vladimir Region (Russia)", *FOTW Flags of the World*, http://www.crwflags.com/FOTW/flags/ru-33.html, accessed 27 June 2008.

Volgograd Oblast
Волгоградская область / Volgogradskaia oblast'

Year Adopted: 2000   **Proportions:** 2:3
Designers: Iu. M. Kurasov and A. V. Shvets

Federal District: Southern
Administrative Center: Volgograd
Population: 2,598,933

Volgograd Oblast's flag has a red field with two narrow blue stripes running vertically at the hoist, creating two additional red stripes—all four the same width. The blue stripes come from the arms of the region, where they run horizontally along the base of the shield. These stripes represent the two major rivers of European Russia—the Volga and the Don. Blue also symbolizes eternal youth and harmony as well as wisdom and spiritual perfection. Red is the historical color of the regiments of the region during the Russian Empire, and recalls the national flag of the Soviet era. It symbolizes courage and steadfastness, and the sacred ground of the region stained by the blood of the defenders of Russia. Centered in the large red area at the fly is a white image of *Rodina-mat' zovet*, which generally translates as "The Motherland Calls". This giant 52-meter statue of Mother Russia commemorates the World War II victory over the Nazis at the Battle of Stalingrad (the Soviet name for Volgograd). The white of the emblem symbolizes peace, nobility, fairness, and blessed ideals.

Sources: "Flag Volgogradskoi oblasti", *Geral'dika.ru*, http://geraldika.ru/symbols/723, accessed 19 June 2008; "Volgogradskaia oblast'", *Vexillographia: Flagi Rossii*, http://www.vexillographia.ru/russia/subjects/volgrad.htm, accessed 1 August 2008; Borisov and Kozina, p. 116; Saprykov (2004), p. 42; Saprykov (2006), p. 41; Smetannikov, p. 51; Solov'ëv, p. 104-105; "Volgograd Region (Russia)", *FOTW Flags of the World*, http://www.crwflags.com/FOTW/flags/ru-34.html, accessed 27 June 2008; "The Motherland Calls," *Wikipedia*, http://en.wikipedia.org/wiki/The_Motherland_Calls, accessed 5 July 2008.

Vologda Oblast
Вологодская область / Vologodskaia oblast'

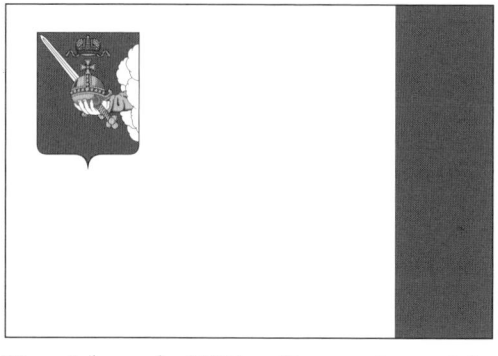

Year Adopted: 1997 **Proportions:** 2:3
Designer: unknown

Federal District: Northwestern
Administrative Center:
  Vologda
Largest City: Cherepovets
Population: 1,218,241

The flag of Vologda Oblast is white with a red vertical stripe along the fly, 1/5 the length of the flag. In the upper hoist are the arms of the oblast, which show a right hand extending out from the clouds. The hand holds a golden cross-bearing orb—a symbol of authority, statehood, and the rights of the oblast as a federal subject of the Russian Federation. Behind the orb is a silver sword with a gold hilt which represents validity, the law, and defense of the fatherland. An imperial Russian crown centered over the orb recalls the historical status of the region. In the arms, red symbolizes authority and courage, gold represents abundance and power, and silver/white stands for nobility, light, and purity.

Sources: Vologodskaia oblast', "Simvolika", http://vologda-oblast.ru/main.asp?V=59&LNG=RUS, accessed 14 June 2008; "Flag Vologodskoi oblasti", *Geral'dika.ru*, http://geraldika.ru/symbols/729, accessed 19 June 2008; "Vologodskaia oblast'", *Vexillographia: Flagi Rossii*, http://www.vexillographia.ru/russia/subjects/vologda.htm, accessed 1 August 2008; Borisov and Kozina, p. 119-120; Saprykov (2004), p. 43; Saprykov (2006), p. 42; Smetannikov, p. 52; Solov'ëv, p. 64-65; "Vologda Region (Russia)", *FOTW Flags of the World*, http://www.crwflags.com/FOTW/flags/ru-35.html, accessed 27 June 2008.

Voronezh Oblast
Воронежская область / Voronezhskaia oblast'

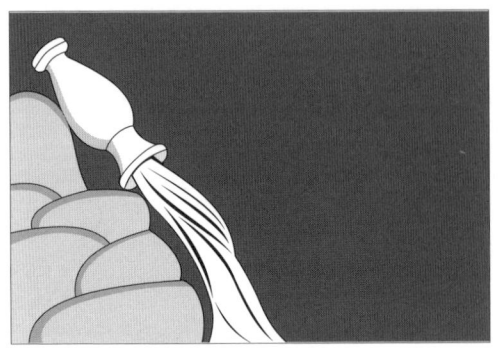

Year Adopted: 2005   **Proportions:** 2:3
Designers: Iu. Korzhik, R. Malanichev, K. Mochënov, M. Medvedev, and O. Afanas'eva

Federal District: Central
Administrative Center: Voronezh
Population: 2,270,031

Voronezh Oblast's flag is red with a mountain of large yellow stones rising from the lower hoist. On the slope of the mountain is an overturned white jug, from which is spilling out a stream of water (also in white). This flag is an armorial banner of the coat of arms where red is symbolic of labor; gold (yellow) represents harvest, light, and spirituality; and silver (white) symbolizes magnanimity. The mountain reflects the geography of the area, the jug is a symbol of the riches and fertility of the region, and the water represents the Voronezh River. The design of the flag was a cooperative effort of the Union of Heraldists of Russia including those individuals listed as the designers.

Another flag, used from 1997 to

2005, was similar to the Russian SFSR flag with a red field and a single blue stripe at the hoist. An earlier version of the oblast's arms was centered in the red area of the flag.

Sources: Voronezhskaia oblast', "Ofitsial'naia simvolika oblasti", http://www.govvrn.ru/wps/wcm/connect/voronezh/AVO/Main/uzel_simv/, accessed 14 June 2008; "Flag Voronezhskoi oblasti", *Geral'dika.ru*, http://geraldika.ru/symbols/13264, accessed 19 June 2008; "Flag Voronezhskoi oblasti (1997 g.)", *Geral'dika.ru*, http://geraldika.ru/symbols/739, accessed 8 August 2008;"Gerb Voronezhskoi oblasti", Geraldika.ru, http://geraldika.ru/symbols/12114, accessed 11 July 2008; "Voronezhskaia oblast'", *Vexillographia: Flagi Rossii*, http://www.vexillographia.ru/russia/subjects/voronezh.htm, accessed 1 August 2008; Borisov and Kozina, p. 129; Saprykov (2004), p. 44; Saprykov (2006), p. 43; Smetannikov, p. 53; Solov'ëv, p. 26-27; "Voronezh Region (Russia)", *FOTW Flags of the World*, http://www.crwflags.com/FOTW/flags/ru-36.html, accessed 27 June 2008.

Yamalo-Nenets Autonomous Okrug
Ямало-Ненецкий автономный округ / Iamalo-Nenetskii avtonomnyi okrug

Year Adopted: 1996 **Proportions:** 2:3
Designer: unknown

Federal District: Urals
Administrative Center: Salekhard
Largest City: Novy Urengoy
Population: 543,651

Yamalo-Nenets Autonomous Okrug (or Yamalia) has a blue flag. Near the bottom of the field are three narrow horizontal stripes of white, blue, and red (in the order of the national flag). Above the white stripe is a repeating ornament of stylized deer antlers, alternating white and blue. Reindeer are a prominent species of the tundra. Blue symbolizes greatness and beauty and is the color of the sky. It also represents the water of the Karsk Sea and the many rivers and lakes in the territory. White is a symbol of purity, good, independence, and the blessed thoughts and intentions of the people. It also represents the long, harsh winters of the region. Red is the color of courage and steadfastness.

Sources: Iamalo-Nenetskii avtonomnii okruga, "Flag i gerb", http://adm.yanao.ru/47/, accessed 15 June 2008; "Flag Iamalo-Nenetskogo avtonomnogo okruga", *Geral'dika.ru*, http://geraldika.ru/symbols/532, accessed 18 June 2008; "Iamalo-Nenetskii avtonmnyi okrug", *Vexillographia: Flagi Rossii*, http://www.vexillographia.ru/russia/subjects/yamal.htm, accessed 1 August 2008; Borisov and Kozina, p. 409; Saprykov (2004), p. 95; Saprykov (2006), p. 95; Smetannikov, p. 106; Solov'ëv, p. 152-153; "Yamal (Russia)", *FOTW Flags of the World*, http://www.crwflags.com/FOTW/flags/ru-yan.html, accessed 27 June 2008.

Yaroslavl Oblast
Ярославская область / Iaroslavskaia oblast'

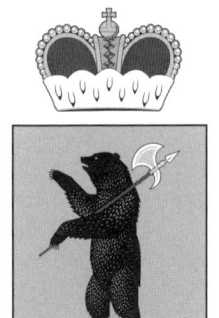

Year Adopted: 2001 **Proportions:** 2:3
Designer: N. V. Koshkin

Federal District: Central
Administrative Center: Yaroslavl
Population: 1,310,473

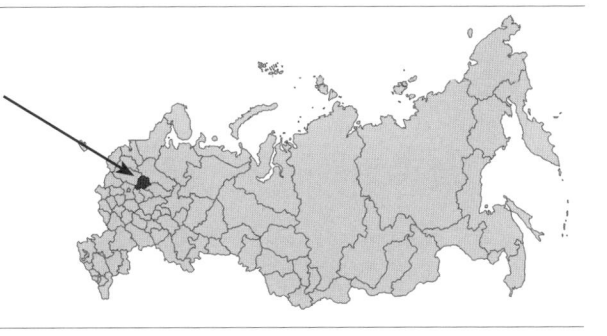

The flag of Yaroslavl Oblast is taken from the field of the oblast's arms. Yellow (gold) is a traditional color to represent the region. Standing in the center of the flag is a black bear holding a poleax in his left paw over his shoulder. The bear comes from the legend of Yaroslav I (the Wise), who founded the city of Yaroslavl. According to the story, when he first arrived in the region, Yaroslav subjugated the pagan population by killing their sacred bear with his halberd.

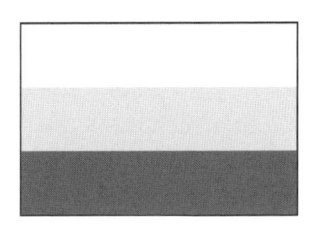

Another design, used from 1998 to 2000, was a horizontal tricolor of white over yellow over green.

Sources: Iaroslavskaia oblast', "Simvolika oblasti", http://www.adm.yar.ru/section.aspx?section_id=111, accessed 15 June 2008; "Flag Iaroslavskoi oblasti", *Geral'dika.ru*, http://geraldika.ru/symbols/94, accessed 20 June 2008; "Flag Iaroslavskoi oblasti (1998 g.)", *Geral'dika.ru*, http://geraldika.ru/symbols/1184, accessed 7 August 2008; "Iaroslavskaia oblast'", *Vexillographia: Flagi Rossii*, http://www.vexillographia.ru/russia/subjects/yaroslav.htm, accessed 1 August 2008; Borisov and Kozina, p. 337-338; Saprykov (2004), p. 82; Saprykov (2006), p. 82; Smetannikov, p. 93; Solov'ëv, p. 52-53; "Yaroslavl Region (Russia)", *FOTW Flags of the World*, http://www.crwflags.com/FOTW/flags/ru-76.html, accessed 27 June 2008.

Zabaikal Krai
Забайкальский край / Zabaikal'skii krai

Year Adopted: 1995; 2009   **Proportions:** 2:3
Designers: L. V. Kulesh and V. I. Kulesh

Federal District: Siberian
Administrative Center: Chita
Population: 1,117,030

The flag of Zabaikal Krai has a yellow triangle at the hoist, extending nearly half-way to the fly, and two horizontal stripes, green over red, at the fly. Together, green and red represent the frontier location of the oblast. Yellow is the traditional color of the Zabaikal Cossacks who defended the eastern boundaries of Russia. Combined, all three colors also symbolize the natural environment of the region—yellow represents the endless steppe, green recalls the taiga and the richness of the wildlife, and red stands for the regions below the surface. The flag was originally adopted in 1995 as the flag of Chita Oblast. After Chita Oblast merged with Agin-Buryat Autonomous Okrug on 1 March 2008 to form Zabaikal Krai, a commission was formed to design new symbols for the krai. On 1 March 2009 the krai formally adopted the design as the flag of Zabaikal Krai.

Sources: "Flag Chitinskoi oblasti", *Geral'dika.ru*, http://geraldika.ru/symbols/1179, accessed 20 June 2008; "Chitinskaia oblast'", *Vexillographia: Flagi Rossii*, http://www.vexillographia.ru/russia/subjects/chita.htm, accessed 1 August 2008; Borisov and Kozina, p. 335; Saprykov (2004), p. 81; Saprykov (2006), p. 81; Smetannikov, p. 92; Solov'ëv, p. 178-179; "Chita Region (Russia)", *FOTW Flags of the World*, http://www.crwflags.com/FOTW/flags/ru-chi.html, accessed 27 June 2008; "U Zabaikal'skogo kraia poka net gerba i flaga," *GTRK Chita* (7 March 2008), http://chita.rfn.ru/rnews.html?id=25951, accessed 24 June 2008; "Sozdana komissiia po razrabotke gerba i flaga", *Regnum Informatsionnoe Agentstvo* (17 March 2008), http://www.regnum.ru/news/972222.html, accessed 24 June 2008; "Flag Zabaikal'skogo kraia", *Vikipediia* (19 May 2008), http://ru.wikipedia.org (direct URL not available), accessed 24 June 2008.

Flag Descriptions: Merged Federal Subjects

As has previously been discussed, some federal subjects have merged since the creation of the Russian Federation. The flags of the merged regions are described in the following section, but were not included in the design analysis. Most of these flags represent autonomous okrugs which merged into the oblast or krai of which they are a part. One of the flags belongs to Kamchatka Oblast, which merged with Koryak Autonomous Okrug to form Kamchatka Krai. The government has formed a commission and held a design contest, but has yet to pick a new flag. In several cases the flags of former federal subjects continue to be used after the mergers, but their status as official symbols is not always clear.

Agin-Buryat Autonomous Okrug
Агинский-Бурятский автономный округ / Aginskii-Buriatskii avtonomnyi okrug
Merged into: Zabaikal Krai

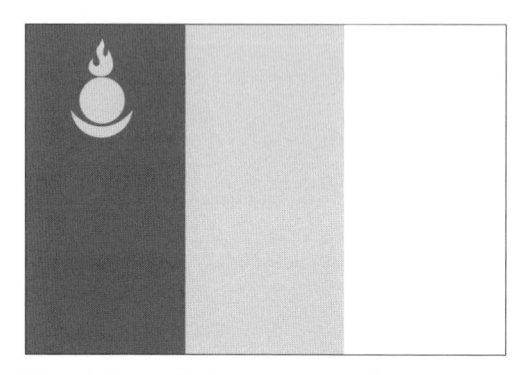

Year Adopted: 2001, 2009   **Proportions:** 2:3
Designer: Bato Galsanovich Dampilon

The flag of Agin-Buryat Autonomous Okrug has three equal vertical stripes—blue, yellow, and white. Centered in the upper hoist is a yellow *soyombo*, a cultural symbol of the Mongol people that combines a flame of the hearth, the sun, and the crescent moon. The symbolism of the *soyombo* is the same as in the flag of Buryatia. Blue represents eternity, freedom, the purity of nature, respect, good relations, peace, and harmony between people. It is also the color of a Mongolian *khadag*—a silk scarf traditionally given to honored guests and elders as a sign of respect, blessing, happiness, and longevity. Yellow is the color of faith and has long been associated with the religion of the people—Buddhism. White symbolizes honesty, purity of thoughts, well-being, wealth, and is reminiscent of the color of dairy foods, which are important to the culture. The *soyombo* was altered in 2009 so that the crescent moon is now narrower and the flame matches the asymmetric version used on the coat of arms.

Another flag, used from 1996 to 2001, had a yellow stripe at the hoist with the *soyombo* in blue. Three horizontal stripes at the fly mirrored the national flag—white/blue/red. The width of the yellow stripe was approximately 1/6 of the length of the flag. This first flag was designed by Batozhargal Shagdarov. On 1 March 2008, the autonomous okrug merged with Chita Oblast to form Zabaikal Krai.

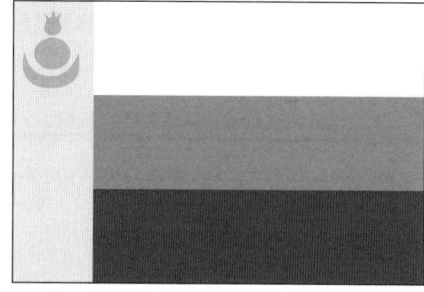

Sources: "Flag Aginskogo Buriatskogo avtonomnogo okruga", *Geral'dika.ru*, http://geraldika.ru/symbols/2038, accessed 18 June 2008; "Aginskii Buriatskii avtonomnyi okrug", *Vexillographia: Flagi Rossii*, http://www.vexillographia.ru/russia/subjects/aginskoe.htm, accessed 1 August 2008; Borisov and Kozina, p. 394; Saprykov (2004), p. 86; Saprykov (2006), p. 86; Smetannikov, p. 97; Solov'ëv, p. 180-181; "Aghin Buriatia (Russia)", *FOTW Flags of the World*, http://www.crwflags.com/FOTW/flags/ru-agb.html, accessed 27 June 2008; "Khata", *Wikipedia*, http://en.wikipedia.org/wiki/Khadag, accessed 12 July 2008; Zakonodatel'noe Sobranie Zabaikal'skogo kraia, "O simvolakh Aginskogo Buriatskogo okruga Zabaikal'skogo kraia," http://oblduma.chita.ru/store/files_v3/zakon_231-zzk.doc, accessed 18 November 2009.

Evenk Autonomous Okrug
Эвенкийский автономный округ / Evenkiiskii avtonomnyi okrug
Merged into: Krasnoyarsk Krai

Year Adopted: 1995   **Proportions:** 1:2
Designer: Sergei Salatkin

Evenk Autonomous Okrug has a flag with three horizontal stripes of light blue, white, and dark blue in proportions of 27:34:27. The stripes represent the colors of the polar day and night, characterizing the northern environment of the okrug. Centered on the white stripe is a *kumalan* emblem with eight spokes, a traditional solar symbol in Evenki culture. Evenk Autonomous Okrug merged into Krasnoyarsk Krai on 1 January 2007.

Sources: "Flag Evenkiiskogo avtonomnogo okruga", *Geral'dika.ru*, http://geraldika.ru/symbols/530, accessed 18 June 2008; Borisov and Kozina, p. 408; Saprykov (2004), p. 94; Saprykov (2006), p. 94; Smetannikov, p. 105; Solov'ëv, p. 186-187; "Evenkia (Russia)", *FOTW Flags of the World*, http://www.crwflags.com/FOTW/flags/ru-eve.html, accessed 27 June 2008; "Flag of Evenk Autonomous Okrug", *Wikipedia*, http://en.wikipedia.org/wiki/Flag_of_Evenk_Autonomous_Okrug, accessed 12 July 2008.

Kamchatka Oblast
Камчатская область / Kamchatskaia oblast'
Merged into: Kamchatka Krai

Year Adopted: 2004 **Proportions:** 2:3
Designer: unknown

Kamchatka Oblast's flag has a white field with a blue stripe at the base, 1/3 the width of the flag. At the upper hoist is an emblem from the arms of the area, which features three erupting volcanoes over alternating wavy lines of blue, white, and blue. The Kamchatka Peninsula has 160 volcanoes, 29 of which are still active. Wavy lines represent the waters which border the region. Blue symbolizes not only the sea, but also the political and economic greatness that Russia has gained from the oceans. White represents a peaceful nature, purity, honor, and nobility. Kamchatka Oblast and Koryak Autonomous Okrug merged on 1 July 2007 to form Kamchatka Krai. A commission for selection of new symbols has held a design contest, but a flag has yet to be adopted. In the meantime, the government website continues to show this flag as that of Kamchatka Oblast.

Sources: "Flag Kamchatskoi oblasti", *Geral'dika.ru*, http://geraldika.ru/symbols/6240, accessed 19 June 2008; "Kamchatskii krai", *Vexillographia: Flagi Rossii*, http://www.vexillographia.ru/russia/subjects/kamcatka.htm, accessed 1 August 2008; Borisov and Kozina, p. 150; Saprykov (2004), p. 48; Saprykov (2006), p. 47; Smetannikov, p. 58; Solov'ëv, p. 198-199; "Kamchatka Territory (Russia)", *FOTW Flags of the World*, http://www.crwflags.com/FOTW/flags/ru-41.html, accessed 27 June 2008.

Komi-Permyak Autonomous Okrug
Коми-Пермяцкий автономный округ /
Komi-Permiatskii avtonomnyi okrug
Merged into: Perm Krai

Year Adopted: 1996   **Proportions:** 1:2
Designers: A. M. Belavin, G. N. Klimova, and V. N. On'kov

The flag of Komi-Permyak Autonomous Okrug has three equal horizontal stripes—red over white over blue. These colors not only represent the colors of the national flag, but are also characteristic of the traditional clothing worn by the Komi-Permyak people. Red also represents courage, strength, bravery, and love. White symbolizes purity of thoughts, innocence, and wisdom. Blue is a symbol of glory, honor, and eternity. It also recalls the sky, bodies of water, and wide open spaces of the territory. Centered on the white stripe is a red symbol from the okrug's arms called a *perna*, formed by the crossing of two sets of parallel lines at a diagonal. This emblem is a widespread cultural symbol that signifies eternity, lofty aspirations, and happiness. The territory merged with Perm Oblast on 1 December 2005 to form Perm Krai.

Sources: "Flag Komi-Permiatskogo avtonomnogo okruga", *Geral'dika.ru*, http://geraldika.ru/symbols/504, accessed 18 June 2008; Borisov and Kozina, p. 395; Saprykov (2004), p. 87; Saprykov (2006), p. 87; Smetannikov, p. 98; Solov'ëv, p. 124-125; "Parma (Russia)", *FOTW Flags of the World*, http://www.crwflags.com/FOTW/flags/ru-81.html, accessed 27 June 2008.

Koryak Autonomous Okrug
Корякский автономный округ /
Koriakskii avtonomnyi okrug
Merged into: Kamchatka Krai

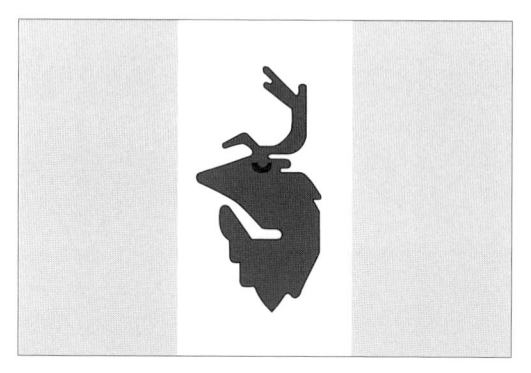

Year Adopted: 1998   **Proportions:** 2:3
Designer: A. V. Prikhod'ko

Koryak Autonomous Okrug's flag has three equal vertical stripes of light blue, white, and light blue. The colors of the flag are drawn from the national flag, and represent unity with Russia, its friendship, and harmony. Light blue is the color of the sky, represents the waters of the Okhotsk Sea and the Bering Sea which wash the shores of the Kamchatka Peninsula, and symbolizes the many rivers in the region. White is tied to the concepts of high moral beginnings, peace, tranquility, well-being, and happiness. It also recalls the climate of the region which is covered in deep snow for much of the year. Centered on the white stripe is the stylized head of a reindeer in red. This represents the basis of rural agriculture in the region—reindeer breeding. The autonomous okrug merged with Kamchatka Oblast on 1 July 2007 to form Kamchatka Krai. A commission for selection of new symbols has held a design contest, but a flag has yet to be adopted. In the meantime, the government website continues to show this flag as that of Koryak Autonomous Okrug.

Sources: "Flag Koriakskogo avtonomnogo okruga", *Geral'dika.ru*, http://geraldika.ru/symbols/512, accessed 18 June 2008; Borisov and Kozina, p. 396; Saprykov (2004), p. 88; Saprykov (2006), p. 88; Smetannikov, p. 99; Solov'ëv, p. 206-207; "Koryakia (Russia)", *FOTW Flags of the World*, http://www.crwflags.com/FOTW/flags/ru-82.html, accessed 27 June 2008.

Taymyr Autonomous Okrug
Таймырский автономный округ /
Taimyrskii avtonomnyi okrug
Merged into: Krasnoyarsk Krai

Year Adopted: 2000 **Proportions:** 2:3
Designer: Vladimir S. Taranets

The flag of Taymyr Automous Okrug is blue. This color symbolizes the greatness and beauty of the Taymyr region, the Yenisei River, and the Kara and Laptev Seas. Centered on the field is a silver/white solar disk with four narrow triangular points extending in the cardinal directions like the four points of a compass. The disk represents the territory of the Taymyr Peninsula and also the long winter which can last for as much as 285 days in the northern regions. It also symbolizes the sun and the warmth it provides to the people of the North. In the center of the disk is a Red-breasted Goose flying from west to east. This goose is a rare bird which nests on the tundra. Its flight path symbolizes the movement of the region toward progress. The Taymyr Automous Okrug merged into Krasnoyarsk Krai on 1 January 2007.

Sources: "Flag Taimyrskogo (Dolgano-Nenetskogo) avtonomnogo okruga", *Geral'dika.ru*, http://geraldika.ru/symbols/516, accessed 18 June 2008; Borisov and Kozina, p. 398; Saprykov (2004), p. 90; Saprykov (2006), p. 90; Smetannikov, p. 101; Solov'ëv, p. 182-183; "Taymyr (Russia)", *FOTW Flags of the World*, http://www.crwflags.com/FOTW/flags/ru-84.html, accessed 27 June 2008.

Ust-Orda Buryat Autonomous Okrug
Усть-Ордынский Бурятский автономный округ /
Ust'-Ordynskii Buriatskii avtonomnyi okrug
Merged into: Irkutsk Oblast

Year Adopted: 1997   **Proportions:** unknown
Designers: M. V. Dambieva, I. I. Soktoeva, A. B. Tsybendorzhieva, and A. A. Bulgatov

The flag of Ust-Orda Buryat Autonomous Okrug (or Ust-Orda Buryatia) has a blue field. Along the bottom of the flag is a white stripe 1/8 the width of the flag, bearing a traditional red pattern from the arts and crafts of the region. In the center of the flag is an emblem from the arms—a gold disk bearing a white triad design with curved beams. Four small gold circles flank the disk at top, bottom, left, and right. This solar symbol represents perfection of the world, the form of the universe, the land, and the ancestral tribe. Blue on the field represents the eternal dark blue of the sky. White symbolizes heaven and the emptiness from which the universe was made, the whiteness of milk, impetus toward development, and the sacred color used in purification and healing rituals. Red symbolizes blood, fire, warmth, the sun, bravery, courage, and fearlessness. Gold represents the richness of the territory. It is also the color of the sun, happiness, and well-being. The Ust-Orda Buryat Autonomous Okrug merged into Irkutsk Oblast on 1 January 2008.

Sources: "Flag Ust'-Ordynskogo Buriatskogo avtonomnogo okruga", *Geral'dika.ru*, http://geraldika.ru/symbols/525, accessed 18 June 2008; Borisov and Kozina, p. 399; Saprykov (2004), p. 91; Saprykov (2006), p. 91; Smetannikov, p. 102; Solov'ëv, p. 184-185; "Ust-Ord Buriatia (Russia)", *FOTW Flags of the World*, http://www.crwflags.com/FOTW/flags/ru-85.html, accessed 27 June 2008.

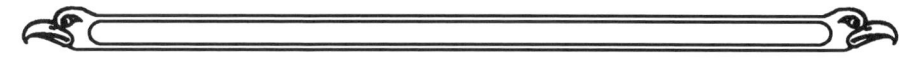

Conclusion

Individually, the flags of the federal subjects each represent a specific region of Russia. The colors, designs, and symbols used are as diverse as the places they represent. While there are some flags that are similar, no dominant design type characterizes Russia's subnational flags. So, as a whole this set of flags is much more distinctive than the subnational flags of some countries, where the majority of the flags can tend to look alike.

Like the blocks of a quilt, the flags combine to tell the story of Russia and its people. A wide variety of cultural symbols illustrate the diversity of the many ethnic groups in the Russian Federation, but common elements also attest to similarities across the cultures. The use of religious symbols of Orthodox Christianity, Islam, Judaism, and Buddhism illustrates one consequence of the Euro-Asian location of Russia, attests to the influence of these faiths on the country as a whole, and demonstrates the resurgence of religion in post-Soviet Russia.

The sometimes chaotic history of Russia is clearly illustrated by the flags and their symbolism. This set of subnational flags unifies a diverse group of territories and peoples, and attests to the achievements of the Russian Empire at its height. Russia spans from Kaliningrad on the Baltic Sea in the west to the eastern coast on the Pacific Ocean. But the story of Russian history is not just one of imperial conquest; it is also one of defense against invasion from the east, from the west, and from the south. The scars of these conflicts on the national psyche, and especially those from the Great Patriotic War (World War II), are evident in the symbolism of the flags. Characteristics such as bravery, courage, steadfastness, and dedication to the defense of the country are repeated over and over again in the meanings of colors and symbols. In addition, more than one period of history is valued in modern Russia. Tsarist emblems and symbols of the Soviet period are recurring themes and have even been combined on several flags, showing that modern Russia has come to terms with the many conflicting elements of its past.

It isn't just the rich history of Russia that is on display in the flag designs. The vast geography of the world's largest country is clearly illustrated in the flags of the federal subjects. They represent the mountains of the Caucasus, the steppe, the taiga, the tundra, the warm regions in the south, and the extreme cold of Siberia and the northern regions. Water is a recurring theme with a vast array of rivers, lakes, and seaports represented on various flags. The richness of the land and bounty of nature that maintain the people are also important themes.

Yet, with all their diversity, one common theme spans this collection of flags. Many of the federal subjects draw upon some or all of the national colors to illustrate their unity with the Russian Federation. This demonstrates that, while each region and each group of people is unique and has its own story to tell, the true story of Russian success comes from the unity of its federal subjects. Together they contribute to the strength of the modern Russian state and will reap the benefits of cooperation to achieve their national goals.

Contributors

Anne M. (Annie) Platoff, author, is the Slavic Studies Librarian at the University of California, Santa Barbara Library. She has been studying Russian for the past six years. To help her learn vexillological terminology in Russian, Annie created a bilingual website— Флаги/Flags (http://russian.platoff.net/flagi/).

While Annie's interest in flags began in childhood, she joined NAVA in 1984. She has twice won the Captain William Driver Award for the best paper presented at the annual meeting of NAVA. This work won in 2008 under the title "Lions and Babrs and Bears: Analyzing the Flags of Russia's Federal Subjects". Annie also won the award in 1992 for "Where No Flag Has Gone Before: Political and Technical Aspects of Placing a Flag on the Moon", which was later published by NASA and in volume 1 of *Raven*. Annie's other vexillological presentations and publications have covered topics such as Soviet children's flags, the use of flags in the U.S. manned space program, the Pike-Pawnee flag incident, and proposed designs for the state flag of Kansas.

Her contributions to NAVA have included serving on the executive board as its second vice president, serving on the editorial board of *Raven*, proofreading every issue of *Raven*, and working on various committees. She has also contributed to an online index of NAVA's publications and is coordinating the creation of NAVA's digital library, which will make these works available to vexillologists around the world.

Annie holds master's degrees in library science from the University of North Texas and historical studies from the University of Houston—Clear Lake. She also has a graduate certificate in museum studies from Arizona State University; her bachelor's degree is in political science and history from Kansas State University.

Edward B. (Ted) Kaye, editor of *Raven* since 1996, is also advisory editor of *The Flag Bulletin*.

A member of NAVA since 1985 and an organizer of the 12th International Congress of Vexillology in 1987, Ted has served as the chief financial officer of a small technology company and as NAVA's treasurer. His articles have appeared in *Raven*, *The Flag Bulletin*, *NAVA News*, the *Vexilloid Tabloid*, and *Flagmaster*, as well as the proceedings of several international congresses. He compiled and published NAVA's guide to flag design *"Good Flag, Bad Flag"*, and has led NAVA's Internet surveys of public perceptions of US and Canadian state/provincial flags and of US city flags.

Colophon

This issue of *Raven: A Journal of Vexillology* was typeset in Adobe Garamond Pro using Adobe InDesign CS3. Typesetting and image processing was performed by Jeanne E. Galick, Graphic Design, Portland, Oregon. The cover design was based on concepts developed by Douglas Lynch.

This journal is printed on 60-pound opaque paper with color plates on 70-pound gloss text paper. Printing and binding was done by Signature Book Printing, Gaithersburg, Maryland www.sbpbooks.com.

Index

abundance:
  green as symbol of, 43, 51-53, 65, 70, 90, 112
  sun as symbol of, 45
  yellow/gold as symbols of, 17, 76, 88, 123
Adygea, Republic of, 16, 24-25, 35, C-2
Adyghe tribes, 35
Agin-Buryat Autonomous Okrug, 128, 130, C-29, C-32
agrarian culture, 80
agriculture:
  animals as symbols of, 135
  grain, 21, 64, 93
  green as symbol, of 93
airplanes, 27-28, 79
Alan culture, 88
Alexander I, standard of, 72
Alexander II:
  flag from the time of, 71
  standard of, 72
Altai Krai, 16, 21, 26, 28, 37, C-2
Altai Republic, 16, 27, 38, C-2
Amur Oblast, 24, 39, C-3
Amur River, 39
ancestors, 52, 56, 66, 110, 137
anchors, 25, 27, 77, 101
Andreevskii flag colors, 16, 38, 40
Angara River, 53
animals, 21-22
  See also specific animals
antiquity, 13-14, 89
Archangel Michael, 19, 22-23, 40
Arctic Ocean, 49
Arkhangelsk Oblast, 16, 19, 22-23, 40, C-3
armor, 40

armorial banners, 10, 41, 78, 83, 101, 113, 124
arrows, 24, 35
arts and crafts, 28-31, 137
aspirations:
  for freedom, 50
  for friendship and cooperation, 58
  for peace, 89
  lofty, 14-15, 57, 134
  spiritual, 93
  to progress, 54
  to revival, 38
  to unity and solidarity, 110
Astrakhan Oblast, 18, 24-25, 41, C-3
atmospheric symbols, 25-26
Aurora Borealis, 25-26, 85
authority, 13-14, 18-19, 101, 123
autonomous oblast and okrugs, 6, 8
Autonomous Soviet Socialist Republics, 7
aviation, 27-28, 79
azure, 14, 40, 54, 58, 95
  See also blue

babr, 22, 53
balance, 82
Balkars, 56
Baltic Sea, 32, 77, 101, 139
banners:
  historical, 87, 100, 104, 110, 115
  of tsars, 72
  See also armorial banners
Bashkortostan, Republic of, 16, 21, 28-29, 42, C-4
battles, 14, 20
  Battle of Stalingrad, 26-27, 121
  Battle of Stara Zagora, 104

battlegrounds, 106
bears, 20-21, 25, 32
   as primary symbol, 24-25, 127
   in arms, 19, 89, 95
beauty:
   blue as symbol of, 14, 51, 57, 63, 65, 85, 91, 93, 95, 97, 126, 136
   of the land, 90, 102, 110
   red as symbol of, 13, 48, 78, 89, 102, 116
   symbols of, 50
   yellow as symbol of, 48
beavers, 22, 53
bees and beehives, 22, 32, 110
Belgorod Oblast, 19, 43, C-4
Bering Sea, 135
BESIK, 15
biblical symbols, 55
   See also Christianity; Judaism
bicolored flags, 12-13
Bii-Khem River, 114
black, 13, 17
   rectangles, 43
   stripes, 76, 118
blades of swords, 24, 28, 113
blast furnaces, 26, 37
blessed ideals and thoughts, 121, 126
blessings, 98, 130
blood, 137
   spilled in battle, 14, 43, 101, 121
blue, 13-16
   crosses, 40, 43
   disks, 58
   fields, 41, 49, 71, 85, 102-103, 114, 126, 136-137
   rectangles, 95
   sinii vs. *goluboi*, 14
   stripes (diagonal), 97
   stripes (horizontal), 38-39, 42, 45, 51, 55-57, 62-63, 65-70, 72, 77, 79-80, 82, 86, 93, 99, 102, 104, 109, 114, 116-117, 119, 126, 132-134
   stripes (narrow) at hoist, 37, 64, 120-121
   stripes (vertical), 37, 53-54, 64, 71, 89-91, 110, 120-121, 130, 135
   waves, 39, 77, 79, 91, 119
   See also azure
boats, 19, 27, 71
bobr, 22, 53

boldness, 14, 104-105
books, 25, 93, 95
boundary regions, 128
bows and arrows, 24, 69
bravery:
   of inhabitants, 51, 95-96, 110
   red as symbol of, 14, 74, 90-91, 93, 97, 120, 134, 137
   symbols of, 69, 98
bread, 90
brotherhood, 17, 66, 78, 102, 116
Bryansk Oblast, 21, 25, 27-28, C-4
Buddhism:
   dairy products used in ceremonies, 15, 43, 114, 130, 137
   lotus flower as symbol of, 20, 58
   yellow as symbol of, 17, 45-46, 58, 130
Bulgarian volunteers (Russo-Turkish War), 104
burial mounds, 26-27, 75
Buryatia (Buryat Republic), 17, 25-26, 28-29, 45-46, 130, C-5

calmness, 14, 62
camels, 21, 27, 32, 48
candlesticks, 25, 89
Caspian Sea, 51
Catherine II (the Great):
   galleon of, 71
   standard of, 72
Caucasus, 56, 62, 140
   mountains, 23, 26, 32, 56, 62
   region, 16, 35
celebration, 78
celestial symbols, 25-26
chalk deposits and manufacturing, 43
Charles XII of Sweden, 43
chastity, 14-15, 104
Chechen national ornament, 29, 47
Chechnya (Chechen Republic), 16, 29-30, 47, C-5
Chelyabinsk Oblast, 21, 27, 48, C-5
Cherkessia, 35
chernozëm, 17, 43, 76
Chita Oblast, 128
Christianity, 19-20
   angels, 22-23, 40
   Gospels, Book of the, 25, 95
   heavenly arms, 23, 69, 98, 123
   icons, 19-20, 94

patron saints, 22, 83-84
    See also crosses
Chukotka Autonomous Okrug, 49, C-6
Chuvashia (Chuvash Republic), 12, 21, 25-26, 29-30, 50, C-6
City of the Cross, 65, 108
clarity, 42
cleanliness, 14-15
    flames as symbol of, 45
    of snow, 70
    of the region, 110
    of the sky, 38, 114
closeness, 62
clothing, traditional, 28-29, 60, 80, 82, 134
clouds, 26, 98, 123
colors, 12-17
    See also names of specific colors
columns, 26, 119
compass points, 136
confidence, 57
consent of the people, 38
constancy, 17, 57, 86, 89
continents, 58
continuity, 13-14, 45, 76, 92, 110
cooperation, 42, 58
cosmos, 118
Cossacks, 58-59, 72, 99, 128
Costumes, national, 28-29, 60, 80, 82, 134
courage:
    inhabitants', 51, 63, 95-96, 98
    red as symbol of, 14, 48, 57, 74, 78, 89-91, 93, 97, 104-105, 110, 120-121, 123, 126, 134, 137
    symbols of, 69, 120
creation, 14, 62, 82
crescent moons, 45, 92, 130
crimson, 50, 72
crosses, 19
    Andreevskii flag, 16, 40
    dividing fields of flags, 10-12, 40, 43, 95
    held by bearers, 89, 120
    Mari El cross, 26, 28, 30, 80
    marking city location, 19, 23, 108
    military cross, 69, 95
    on books, 95
    on crowns, 41, 95, 120, 123
    on orbs, 123
    Orthodox, 20, 92, 95
    St. Andrew's, 16, 40
    St. George's, 95
    Scandinavian, 108
crowns, 18-19
    as crests on arms, 40, 54, 72, 74, 76, 87, 92, 95, 104-106, 110, 112, 119, 120, 124
    as primary symbols on flags, 41, 60, 115
    as symbols in arms, 123
    fashioned from reindeer antlers, 29, 31, 68, 116-117
    in the form of a stylized full bowl, 64
    on double-headed eagles, 93, 101, 108
    worn by animals, 120
cultural symbols, 28-32, 139
    Chechen national ornament, 29-30, 47
    clothing decorations, 29
    embroidery motifs, 29-30
    kumalan, 132
    kurai flower, 28-29, 42
    Mari El cross, 28, 30, 80-81
    perna, 134
    reindeer antler ornaments, 29, 31, 68, 86, 116-117, 126
    solar signs, 28-30, 52, 66-67, 80-82, 118, 132, 137
    soyombo, 20-21, 26, 28-29, 45, 130
    Tree of Life, 29-30, 50

Dagestan, Republic of, 16, 51, C-6
dairy products, 15, 43, 114, 130, 137
dams, hydroelectric, 79
deer, 21, 87
    antlers, 29, 31, 68, 86, 116-117, 126
defense:
    Andreevskii flag as symbol of, 40
    armed figures as symbols of, 40, 100
    fortresses as symbols of, 57, 77, 93
    of Russia in the past, 32, 39, 43, 57, 90, 121, 128, 139
    preparedness, 14, 32, 57, 60, 98
    red as symbol of, 14, 39, 43, 57, 90, 121
    weapons as symbols of, 41, 69, 123
democracy, 13-14, 51
demons, 40
dependability, 93
development, 52, 78, 137
devotion, 89, 90
diagonally-divided flags, 10-11, 97
disks, 26, 49, 58, 102, 136, 137
Don River, 121

146 *Russian Regional Flags*

double-headed eagle, 18, 21-22
   in arms, 93, 108
   on a banner, 18-19
   on a scepter, 101
dragons, 18, 22, 83-84, 108
durability, 17, 57

eagles, 18-19, 21-22
   as prow decorations, 71
   double-headed, 72, 93, 101, 108
   in arms, 43, 54, 72
Earth, movement of, 52
economy and economic development, 13-14, 39, 78-79, 133
education and educational force, 51, 54
Elizabeth Petrovna, Empress, monogram of, 57
embroidery, 28-30, 63
   See also solar signs; reindeer antlers
emptiness, 137
energy, 14, 111
environment:
   natural, 63, 97, 128
   northern, 15, 32, 70, 102, 132, 140
   riches of, 70
equality, 70
eternal dark blue of the sky, 137
eternal life, 17, 35, 42, 66, 94
eternal movements of Sun and Earth, 52
eternal youth, 121
eternity, 38, 80, 130, 134
Evenk Autonomous Okrug, 132, C-30
evil, 40

fairness, 14-15, 80, 89, 121
faith, 17, 90, 130
faithfulness, 14-15, 69, 110
faultlessness, 69, 104, 110
fauna, 53
   See also animals; names of specific animals
fearlessness:
   of the inhabitants, 95-96
   red as symbol of, 14, 60, 74, 91, 93, 97, 105, 137
feats, 97
federal cities, 6, 8, 83, 101
federal subjects, 5-9, 31
feelings, 13, 48

fertility:
   blue as symbol of, 82
   green as symbol of, 17, 43, 52, 62, 69, 72,
   symbols of, 80, 124
   yellow as symbol of, 17, 78
fidelity, 48, 97, 104
field colors, 12-17
field design, 10-12
fields (land), 16, 94
fire, 14, 48, 137
   See also flames
fish and fishing, 22, 32, 79, 89, 105
flags as symbols, 19, 71-72, 92
flames, 45, 130
   See also fire
flora, 16, 53, 65
   See also flowers; grain; trees
flowers, 20-21, 28, 42, 58
folk arts, 80
forests and woods, 16, 44, 53, 63, 68-69, 94, 116
fortresses, 26, 57, 72, 77, 93, 108
fragility of the land, 15
frankness, 15, 104, 112
freedom:
   aspirations for, 50
   blue as symbol of, 14, 102, 130
   green as symbol of, 17, 35, 42, 56, 112
French invasion of Russia (1812), 106
friendliness and friendship:
   green as symbol of, 17, 66, 102
   national colors as symbols of, 135
   symbols of, 42, 57-58,
frontier locations, 128
fur-bearing animals:
   martens, 21, 32, 92
   sables, 21, 32, 53, 90
future, 45, 56, 58

galleons, 27, 71
gamayun, 22, 106
gates, 57
Geese, Red-breasted, 136
generations and ancestors, 52, 56, 66, 110, 137
gentleness, 14, 65, 91, 95, 97
geography and geographic symbols, 23-24, 32, 124
glory, 56, 109, 134

goats, 21, 104
gold (color), iv, 17
   from historical standards, 115
   symbol of abundance, grain, or harvest, 76, 78, 123-124
   symbol of riches or wealth, 85, 114, 116-117, 137
   symbol of sunny region, 108
gold (metal), 17, 79
golden ear and golden fleece, 108
good, 15, 40, 55, 103, 126
good fortune, 17, 88
good relations, 130
goodness, 53, 56, 65, 69, 80, 82, 95
Gospels, Book of the, 25, 95
grain, 21, 28, 37, 64, 78, 93
Great Northern War (1700-21), 101
Great Patriotic War (1939-45), 26-27, 35, 76, 106, 121
greatness:
   blue as symbol of, 51, 63, 65, 91, 93, 97, 110, 126, 133, 136
   yellow/gold as symbols of, 17, 48, 57, 114
green, 13, 16-17
   fields, 35
   rectangles, 43
   stripes (horizontal), 42, 47, 51-52, 55-56, 60, 62-63, 68-70, 72, 75, 86, 102, 109, 111, 116-117, 128
   stripes (vertical), 66-67, 90, 94
   triangles, 65
gun carriages, 25, 106

halberds, 24, 127
hammers:
   and picks, 25, 64, 79
   and shovels, 25
   and sickles, 25, 28, 44, 120
   and sword blades, 28, 113
hand of blessing, 98
happiness:
   blue as symbol of, 14, 58
   green as symbol of, 63
   symbols of, 55, 106, 130, 134
   white as symbol of, 15, 45, 89, 135
   yellow/gold as symbols of, 17, 137
harmony, 135
   blue as symbol of, 14, 114, 121, 130
   red as symbol of, 52
   symbols of, 78

   yellow as symbol of, 45-46
harvest, 17, 94, 124
healing rituals, 137
health:
   green as symbol of, 17, 69, 94, 109
   red as symbol of, 14, 48
   yellow as symbol of, 17
hearths, 45, 130
heaven, 15, 116, 137
   heavenly arms, 23, 69, 98, 123
heraldry:
   authority, 34
   errors, 53
   influence on flags, 9-10, 31
heroism, 57, 90
hills, 23, 78
history, 39, 57, 89, 119
hoist triangles, 10-11
home, 110
   keeper of the, 45
honesty, 14-15, 69, 97, 104, 130
honor, 14-15, 56, 109, 133-134
hope:
   blue as symbol of, 14, 102,
   green as symbol of, 17, 35, 53, 56, 60, 63, 65, 69-70, 86, 90, 112, 116
horizontal stripes, 11
horses, 21, 83-84, 100, 112
hospitality, 57
hydroelectric dams, 26, 28, 79

icons, 20, 23, 94
ideals, 121
Image of Edessa, 20, 94
impenetrability, 106
imperial symbols, 18-19
   banners, flags, and standards, 43, 71-72, 92
   crowns, 41, 60, 72, 76, 92, 112, 115, 119, 123
   double-headed eagle, 72, 93, 101, 108
   galleon, 71
   monograms, 57, 72
   orbs, 18-19, 23, 41, 123
   princes, 100
   sceptors, 57, 89, 101
   thrones, 115
independence, 103, 126
industry, industriousness, and industrial development, 13, 48, 64, 78, 110

148 *Russian Regional Flags*

infinity, 52, 86
Ingushetia, Republic of, 16, 26, 28-30, 52, C-7
innocence, 15, 65, 109, 134
integrity, 45
intentions, 126
interconnection, 52
inviolability, 45
Irkutsk Oblast, 22, 53, 137, C-7
Irtush River, 91
Islam:
   crescent moon, 20, 92
   green as symbol of, 16, 35, 47, 51-52,
islands, 23, 103
Ivanovo Oblast, 24, 54, C-7

Jesus, 20, 23, 94
Jewish Autonomous Oblast, 8, 12, 20, 26, 55, C-8
Jewish symbols, 55
joy, 17, 53, 65, 69, 112
Judaism, 8, 20, 55
jugs, 124
justice, 48, 52, 91

Kaa-Khem River, 114
Kabardino-Balkaria (Kabardino-Balkar Republic), 16, 23, 56, C-8
Kabardins, 56
Kaliningrad Oblast, 19, 26-27, 57, C-8
Kalmuks, 58, 99
Kalmykia, Republic of, 17, 20-21, 58-59, C-9
Kaluga Oblast, 18, 60, C-9
Kama River, 95
Kamchatka Krai, 61, 129, 133, 135
Kamchatka Oblast, 61, 129, 133, C-30
Kamchatka Peninsula, 133, 135
Kara Sea, 136
Karachay-Cherkessia (Karachay-Cherkess Republic), 16, 23, 26, 62, C-10
Karelia, Republic of, 63, C-10
Karelo-Finnish SSR, 63
Karsk Sea, 126
Kemerovo Oblast, 16, 21, 27, 64, C-10
keys, 25, 77
Khabarovsk Krai, 65, C-11
khadag, 130
Khakassia, Republic of, 26, 28-30, 66-67, C-11, C-32

Khanty-Mansi Autonomous Okrug, 29, 31, 68, 116-117, C-11
Kirov Oblast, 19, 23-24, 26, 69, C-12
knowledge, 17, 54, 94, 106
Komi-Permyak Autonomous Okrug, 96, 134, C-30
Komi Republic, 70, C-12
Koryak Autonomous Okrug, 61, 129, 133, 135, C-31
Kostroma Oblast, 16, 18-19, 27, 54, 71, C-12, C-32
krais, 6-7
Krasnodar Krai, 18-19, 26-27, 72-73, C-13, C-32
Krasnoyarsk Krai, 27-28, 74, 132, 136, C-13
Kuban, 72
kumalan, 132
kurai flower, 42
Kurgan Oblast, 26-27, 75, C-13
kurgans, 26-27, 75
Kuril archipelago, 103
Kursk Oblast, 76, 78, C-14
Kuzbass and Kuznetsk Basin, 64
Kyzyl, 114

labor, 13, 57, 80, 124
lakes, 14, 38. 63, 68, 89-90, 95, 116, 126, 140
   Lake Baikal, 53
Lamaism, 45-46
lances, 24, 83-84
land, 17, 118, 137
Laptev Sea, 136
law, 123
leadership, 104, 114
Leningrad Oblast, 12, 15, 24, 26-27, 77, C-14
life:
   eternity of, 35, 42, 66,
   green as symbol of, 16-17, 51, 109
   red as symbol of, 14, 48, 82, 85, 91, 111, 116, 118
   symbols of, 45
   white as symbol of, 80
   yellow as symbol of, 50
light:
   silver as symbol of, 17, 60, 123
   symbols of, 45
   white as symbol of, 15, 60, 123

yellow as symbol of, 94, 124
linden trees, 78
lions, 21, 43, 54, 74, 119-120
Lipetsk Oblast, 21, 23, 78, C-14
literature, 93
lofty aspirations, 57, 134
lofty ideals, 116
lofty purposes, 114
longevity, 48, 130
lotus flowers, 58
love:
    blue as symbol of, 14, 57
    red as symbol of, 13, 48, 91, 104-105, 134
    white as symbol of, 15, 38
loyalty:
    blue as symbol of, 14-15, 45, 56, 85, 109
    red as symbol of, 14, 102
    symbols of, 93

Magadan Oblast, 24, 26-28, 79, C-15
magnanimity:
    red as symbol of, 13, 104-105, 110
    symbols of, 120
    white as symbol of, 48, 91, 124
maps as symbols, 23, 108
Mari El Cross, 26, 28-30, 80-81
Mari El Republic, 26, 28-30, 80-81, C-15, C-32
martens, 21, 32, 92
maturity, 14, 111
meadows, 16, 66
medals, 27, 74
memory, 48
menorahs, 55
mercilessness to enemies, 106
mercy, 13, 45-46, 48, 91
might, 106
Mikhail I Fedorovich (Romanov), 41
military crosses, 69
military ribbons, 27, 74, 100
    Order of Lenin, 27, 44, 64, 72, 74, 106, 110
    Partisans of the Patriotic War, 27, 44
military skill, 69
military valor, 14, 88
milk, 15, 43, 114, 137
minerals and mining, 17, 43, 48-49, 64, 79
modesty, 15, 53, 69
Mongol people, 130

monograms, 57, 72
Monomakh's cap, 115
monuments, 22-23, 26-27, 119, 121
moons, 20-21, 25-26, 45, 92, 130
moral beginnings, 45, 135
morality and morals, 15, 80
Mordovia, Republic of, 26, 28-30, 82, C-15
Mordvin people, 82
Mordvinia, 82
mortars, 25, 44
Moscow (city), 8, 15, 18-19, 22, 24, 27, 83-84, C-16
Moscow Oblast, 19, 22, 24, 27, 84, C-16
Mother Russia, 22, 121
motives, good, 62
Mount Elbrus, 23, 56, 62
mountains, 23-24, 38, 51, 124
    Caucasus range, 23, 26, 32, 56, 62, 140
    Ural Mountains, 48
Murmansk Oblast, 25-26, 85, C-16
musical instruments, 49
Muslim symbolism:
    crescent moon, 20, 92
    green, 16, 35, 47, 51-52,
mutual respect, 114
mythical birds, 106

Napoleonic Wars, 106
nature, 52, 62, 78, 86, 94
    natural environment, 35, 97, 128
naval symbols, 40
Nenets Autonomous Okrug, 29, 31, 86, C-17
Nenetsia, 86
Neva River, 101
Nicholas I, standard of, 72
Nizhny Novgorod Oblast, 87, C-17
nobility:
    of morals, 114
    symbols of, 18-19
    white as symbol of, 15, 48, 91, 104-5, 112, 119, 121, 123, 133

North Ossetia-Alania, Republic of, 88, C-17
northern lights, 25-26, 85
northern regions, 15, 26, 32, 70, 85, 102, 132, 140
Novgorod Oblast, 18, 89, C-18
Novosibirsk Oblast, 21, 27, C-18

150 *Russian Regional Flags*

oblasts, 6-7
oceans, 14, 103, 133, 139
    Arctic Ocean, 49
    Pacific Ocean, 49
Oka River, 60
Okhotsk Sea, 135
omniscience, 94
Omsk Oblast, 24, 91, C-18
open spaces, 70, 134
openness, 42, 82
orange, 55
orbs, 18-19, 23, 41, 123
Order of Lenin, 27
    field of flag, 106
        ribbon in arms, 44, 64, 72, 74, 110
Orenburg Oblast, 19-20, 26, 92, C-19
Orthodox symbolism, 19-21, 60, 92, 94
Oryol Oblast, 21, 25-26, 78, C-19
Ottoman Turks, 104
outlook, 94

Pacific Ocean, 49
pan-Slavic colors, 15
Partisans of the Patriotic War, 27, 44
partridges, 22, 32, 76
past, 45, 89
patience, 48
Paul I, standard of, 72
peace:
    aspirations for, 89
    blue as symbol of, 14, 57, 62, 130
    green as symbol of, 17, 60
    of mind, 86
    symbols of, 20, 55, 106
    white as symbol of, 15, 45, 80, 95, 109, 116, 119, 121, 135
    yellow as symbol of, 17
peaceful disposition or nature, 42, 56, 133
Penza Oblast, 12, 19-20, 23, 94, C-19
people as symbols, 18, 69, 100
perfection, 15, 50, 116, 137
Perm Krai, 19, 25, 95-96, 134, C-20
Perm Oblast, 96
perna, 134
Peter I (the Great), 15, 43, 115
phoenix, 106
picks, 25, 64, 79
pitchers, 25, 124
planetary movement, 52
plants, 21

plenty, 17, 35, 78
polar regions, 132
polearms, 127
Polish–Muscovite War (1605–18), 106
power, 17, 57, 123
present, 45
Priamurye, 39
Primorsky Krai, 21, 97, C-20
princes, 100
progress, 13, 54, 85, 102, 136
proportions, 11-12, 31
prosperity:
    green as symbol of, 17, 78
    symbols of, 52, 58, 79, 106
    yellow/gold as symbols of, 17
Pskov Oblast, 98, C-20
purity, 14-15
    blue as symbol of, 14, 85
    of actions, 52
    of intentions, 15, 82
    of morals, 69, 88, 118
    of nature and the environment, 15, 130
    of temperaments, 102
    of thoughts, 15, 17, 42, 52-53, 55, 60, 65, 76, 82, 93, 95, 102, 105, 130, 134
    purification rituals, 137
    white as symbol of, 48-49, 65, 86, 90-91, 95, 103, 109, 111, 114, 116, 119, 123, 126, 133
purple, 50, 55

quartered flags, 10-11

railroads, 27, 90
rainbows, 20, 26, 55
red, 13-16
    fields, 37, 39, 44, 48, 64, 74, 78-79, 83-84, 92-93, 101, 106, 113, 120-121, 124
    rectangles, 43, 95
    stripes (diagonal), 97
    stripes (horizontal), 39, 47-48, 50-51, 55, 57, 60, 62-63, 66-67, 72, 76-77, 80, 82, 85, 88, 99-100, 102, 104-106, 111, 119, 126, 128, 134
    stripes (vertical), 54, 64, 71, 89-91, 110, 115, 118, 121, 123
    triangles, 116-117
    waves, 77
    See also crimson

Red-breasted Geese, 136
regimental standards, 100
registration of symbols, 34
reindeer, 126, 135
reindeer antlers:
    as crown ornaments, 29, 31, 68, 116-117
    as repeating patterns, 29, 31, 86, 126
religions:
    pre-Christian, 19, 80, 95, 127
    resurgence of, 19-20, 32
    symbolism of, 19-21, 26, 32
    See also Buddhism; Christianity; Islam; Judaism; Lamaism
renewal, 17, 109, 116
republics, 6-7
respect, 14-15, 114, 130
restraint, 62
retribution toward enemies, 106
revival:
    green as symbol of, 17, 66, 90, 102, 111
    symbols of, 45, 50, 94
    white as symbol of, 38
ribbons, 27, 37, 74, 100
riches and richness:
    agricultural, 43, 94
    blue as symbol of, 38, 53, 63, 68, 89-90, 95, 116, 126, 135
    green as symbol of, 62, 72
    of nature, the environment, and the region, 53, 69-70, 72, 109, 124, 128, 137
    yellow/gold as symbol of, 114
    See also wealth
rivers, 14, 24, 32
    Amur River, 24, 39
    Angara River, 53
    Don River, 121
    Irtush River, 24, 91
    Kama River, 95
    Neva River, 101
    Ob' River, 90
    Oka River, 60
    Volga River, 24, 41, 54, 71, 119, 121
    Voronezh River, 24, 124
    Vyatka River, 69
    Yenisei River, 115, 136
roads, 108
Rodina-mat' zovet, 22-23, 121
Romanov Dynasty, 41
Rostov Oblast, 99, C-21

RSFSR flag colors, 14, 16, 27-28, 37, 64, 71, 120, 124-125
Rus, the, 115
Russian Empire, 8-9, 20, 76
Russian Federation, 5-9, 18
    arms, 18, C-1
    flag, 11, 13-16, 31, C-1
Russian language, 2-3, 5, 13-17, 22
Russian national arms, 18, C-1
Russian national flag, 11, 13-16, 31, C-1
Russian national symbols, 5, 15, 18-19, 31
Russian navy, 16, 40
Russian Orthodoxy, 19-20, 60, 92, 94
Russian soldiers, 57
Russian Soviet Federative Socialist Republic:
    flag colors of, 14, 16, 27-28, 37, 64, 71, 120, 124-125
    flag of, 9, 27-28
    subdivisions of, 7, 9
Russian tricolor, 11-12, 15-16, 31, 49, C-1
Russians (ethnicity), 5, 82, 99
Russians (nationality), 5
Russo-Turkish War (1877-78), 104
Ryazan Oblast, 18, 22-23, 78, 100, C-21

sables, 21, 32, 53, 90
sacrifices, 97
St. Andrew:
    cross of, 16, 40
    ribbon of, 87, 104, 120
St. George:
    cross of, 95
    in the arms of Russia, 108, C-1
    symbol of Moscow, 15, 18-19, 22, 24, 83-84
St. Petersburg, 8, 18, 27, 101, C-21
Sakha Republic (Yakutia), 25-26, 102, C-22
Sakhalin Island, 103
Sakhalin Oblast, 23, 103, C-22
salt, 90
Samara banner, 104
Samara Oblast, 104, C-22
Saratov Oblast, 105, C-23
Scandinavian crosses, 108
scepters, 18, 57, 89, 101
scimitars, 24-25, 41
sculptures, 22-23, 26-27
Scythians, 88

seas, 14, 23, 49, 133, 139
  Baltic Sea, 32, 77, 101
  Bering Sea, 135
  Caspian Sea, 51
  Kara Sea, 136
  Karsk Sea, 126
  Laptev Sea, 136
  Okhotsk Sea, 135
  ports, 40, 77, 101, 140
  waves, 103, 133
selflessness, 14, 57
shovels, 25, 74
shuttles, 25, 54
Siberia, 32, 97, 140
  green as symbol of, 66, 75
  white as symbol of, 75, 91, 103
  winters in, 53, 90-91
sickles, 25, 28, 74, 120
silver (color), iv, 13, 17
  stripes, 60, 76
  waves and water, 24, 54, 124
silver (metal), 79
sincerity, 14-15, 56, 109
sky:
  blue as symbol of, 14, 80, 102, 114, 116, 126, 134-135, 137
  cleanliness of, 38, 80
  white as symbol of, 65
Smolensk Oblast, 25, 27, 106-107, C-23
snow, 15, 49, 53, 68-70, 102, 116, 135
snow leopards, 98
solar disks, 45, 102, 130, 136-137
solar signs, 26, 28-30
  circular, 52, 66-67, 132, 136-137
  cross-like, 80-82, 118, 134
  kumalan, 132
  Mari El cross, 26, 28-30, 80-81
  perna, 134
solid fields, 10-11
Soviet Union:
  breakup of, 5, 15, 83
  colors used by, 13-14, 16, 121
  flags of, 9, 14, 16, 24, 63, 76, 120-121
  subdivisions, of 7, 44, 63
  symbols of, 21, 25, 83, 120
  symbols retained from, 27-28, 44, 120
soyombo, 20-21, 26, 28, 45, 130
Spas Nerukotvornyi, 20, 23, 94
spiritual aspirations, 93
spiritual beginnings and origins, 45-46, 80

spiritual perfection, 45-46, 121
spirituality:
  symbols of, 94
  white as symbol of, 15, 82, 105
  yellow/gold as symbol of, 17, 124
spring, 111
stability, 17, 78, 82, 93, 118
Stalingrad, Battle of, 121
standards, regimental, 100
Stara Zagora, Battle of, 104
stars, 25-26, 29, 35, 50
statehood, 123
statues, 22-23, 26-27, 121
Stavropol Krai, 19, 23, 26, 108, C-23
steadfastness, 14, 57, 110, 121, 126
steppe, 16, 66, 128, 140
stones, 124
strength:
  red as symbol of, 14, 48, 57, 60, 63, 111, 116, 134
  symbols of, 40, 98, 104, 120
stripes, 10-11
structures, 26
sturgeons, 105
succession, 45
sugar, 43
summer, 102
sun:
  and solar system, 52
  red as symbol of, 14, 118, 137
  solar disks, 25-26, 45, 102, 130, 136, 137
  solar symbols, 26, 28-30, 52, 66-67, 80-82, 118, 132, 134, 136-137
  sunny regions, 108
  sunrises, 62
  white sun, 102
  yellow/gold as symbols of, 50, 58, 78, 137
Sverdlovsk Oblast, 6, 109, C-24, C-32
Sweden, 43
swords:
  blades of, 24-25, 113
  held or worn by figures, 24, 40, 100, 121, 123
  scimitars, 24-25, 41
symbols, 11, 18-32

taiga, 16, 65-66, 70, 102, 128
Tambov Oblast, 27, C-24

Tatars, 82, 112
Tatarstan, Republic of, 16, 111, C-24
Taymyr Autonomous Okrug, 136, C-31
tea, 114
textile industry, 54
thoughts, 126
thrift, 110
thrones, 89, 115
tigers, 21-22, 32, 53, 97
Tomsk Oblast, 112, C-25
tools, 25
    See also names of specific tools
torches, 25, 54
tranquility, 15, 45, 135
transliteration, 2, 32
transportation, 27, 48, 79
Trans-Siberian Railway, 27, 90
Tree of Life, 21, 29, 50
trees, 21, 44, 50, 78
triad, 137
triangles, 10-11, 49, 65, 116, 128
tribar and tricolor flags, 11-13
truth and truthfulness, 15, 105, 116
Tsarina of vases, 37
tsarist symbols, 18-19
Tula Oblast, 24-25, 28, 113, C-25
tundra, 126, 136, 140
Turkic peoples, 102
Tuva Republic, 17, 114, C-25
Tuvans, 114
Tver Oblast, 18, 115, C-26
Tyumen Oblast, 18, 29, 31, 116-117, C-26
Tyva Republic, 17, 114, C-25

Udmurtia (Udmurt Republic), 26, 28-30, 118, C-26
Ulug-Khem River, 114
Ulyanovsk Oblast, 15, 24, 26, 119, C-27
underground regions, 128
understanding, 56
unity, 45
    of ethnicities, 42, 70, 82
unity with Russia:
    Andreevskii flag colors as symbol of, 38, 45
    crowns as symbol of, 41, 106
    flags as symbols of, 92
    maps as symbols of, 103
    national flag colors as symbol of, 66, 95, 97, 99, 119, 126, 135
    red as symbol of, 116
    RSFSR flag colors as symbol of, 37, 120
    2-headed eagles as symbol of, 93
universe, 66, 137
Ural mountains and region, 48, 109
USSR *See* Soviet Union
Ust-Orda Buryat Autonomous Okrug, 137, C-31

validity, 123
valor, 14, 88
vertical stripes, 11
veterans, 76
victories:
    military, 27, 32, 97, 122
    over paganism, 127
Virgin Mary, belt of, 60
virtue, 14-15, 42
vitality:
    flames as symbol of, 45
    green as symbol of, 17, 86, 90
    red as symbol of, 14, 57, 78, 102
Vladimir Oblast, 16, 18, 28, 54, 120, C-27
volcanoes, 133
Volga River, 41, 54, 71, 119, 121
Volga-Urals region, 16
Volgograd, 121
Volgograd Oblast, 19, 22-23, 26-27, 121-122, C-27
Vologda Oblast, 18, 23, 26, C-28
Voronezh Oblast, 16, 23-24, 78, 124-125, C-28, C-32
Voronezh River, 124
Vyatka River, 69

walls, 77
warmth:
    flames as symbols of, 14, 45
    of human relationships, 95
    red as symbol of, 14, 62, 137
    solar signs as symbols of, 82, 136
wars, 32, 139
    French invasion of Russia (1812), 106
    Great Northern War (1700-21), 101
    Great Patriotic War (1939-45), 26-27, 35, 76, 106, 121, 139
    Polish-Muscovite War (1605-18), 106
    Russo-Turkish War (1877-78), 104
    World War II (1939-45), 26-27, 35, 76, 106, 121, 139

water, 24, 32
  blue as symbol of, 63, 65, 68, 80, 89, 95, 103, 126, 134-135
  pouring from a jug, 124
  waves as symbols of, 54, 77, 79, 91, 119, 133
wealth:
  mineral, 17
  symbols of, 45, 106
  white as symbol of, 130
  yellow as symbol of, 17, 57, 78, 85, 116
weapons, 24-25
  held by figures, 24-25, 40, 69, 83-84, 100, 119, 121, 123, 127
  manufacture of, 113
  primary symbols, 35, 41
  symbols in arms, 40, 44, 69, 106, 119, 123
welcoming guests, 90, 114, 130
well-being:
  blue as symbol of, 14, 110
  symbols of, 45, 52, 58, 79
  white as symbol of, 15, 45, 89. 130, 135
  yellow/gold as symbols of, 17, 137
wheat, 64
white, 13, 15-17
  crosses, 95, 108
  disks, 136
  fields, 38, 40, 52-53, 55, 69, 75, 77, 86-87, 89, 105, 112, 119, 123, 133
  rectangles, 43
  stripes (diagonal), 97
  stripes (horizontal), 38-39, 42, 45, 47, 52, 54-56, 60, 65-67, 69-70, 75, 77, 79-80, 82, 86, 88, 100, 102, 104-105, 109, 111, 114, 116-117, 119, 126, 132-134, 137
  stripes (vertical), 47, 53, 68, 89-91, 99, 118, 130, 135

triangles, 49
waves, 39, 54, 77, 79, 119
winter, 15, 49, 53, 69, 90, 126, 136
wisdom:
  blue as symbol of, 121
  green as symbol of, 17, 62
  symbols of, 48, 106, 116
  white as symbol of, 15, 134
  yellow as symbol of, 17, 94
woods and forests, 16, 44, 53, 63, 68-69, 94, 116
work and workers, 44, 78
World War II (1939-45), 26-27, 35, 76, 106, 121
wreaths, 21, 37, 105, 120

Yakut people, 102
Yakutia, 25-26, 102
Yamalia, 126
Yamalo-Nenets, A.O., 29, 31, 116-117, 126, C-28
yarar, 49
Yaroslav the Wise, 24-25, 127
Yaroslavl Oblast, 21, 24-25, 127, C-29, C-32
yellow, 13, 16-17
  disks, 49, 137
  fields, 50, 58, 94, 108, 115, 127
  stripes (horizontal), 45, 48, 50, 55, 57, 76, 88, 99-100, 106
  stripes (vertical), 115, 130
  triangles, 114, 128
Yenisei River, 115, 136
youth, 17, 60, 62, 86, 116, 121

Zabaikal Krai, 128, C-29